I Give You Two Weeks

A simple yes, that led to an everlasting change

By: Jesse Garcia

For more information visit: www.twoweeks.org

CONTENTS

Chapter 1 – Gods Plan

Night fell quickly as the dark Georgia sky grew heavy. The clouds rumbled as I looked over to my sister and said, "hey, we should probably get going, its getting late." She shrugged me off as I continued… "we have school tomorrow, and dad is going to get mad." Sister - "Ok, ok, let's go" as she looked over to her boyfriend and said goodbye. We ran all the way home and tried to avoid as many rain drops as we could. I unlocked the door and noticed that all the lights were out. Sister – "I thought dad was home?" Jesse – "So did I, maybe he's still out doing laundry?" We turned the lights on and went to our rooms. After a couple of minutes, I heard a tapping coming from the living room - "it's probably the thunder or rain" I thought to myself. About ten minutes passed and I kept hearing the same sound. I slowly got out of my bed and headed toward the living room. I waited there to see if I could hear the sound again. "Tap tap," There it was again! I pushed the curtain to the right and took a peak outside. As I looked out, I saw my dad holding a white laundry bag over his shoulder. I unlocked the door and slid the glass door open and said, "Dad why are you on the porch?" Dad - "I forgot to take my keys when I went to get the laundry from down the street. I thought you and your sister were staying home for the night..." My heart sunk to the bottom of my stomach - "I'm so sorry... I promise it won't..." Before I could finish my sentence, he interrupted me and said, "Its ok. I stood outside and listened to the rain and the thunder. It's a beautiful night, right?" Jesse - "Uh, yeah... I mean yes!!" I was shocked. I didn't understand. Why is he not mad? I thought he was going to be at least a little upset. Growing up I saw my dad in many moments where I did not understand the way he reacted. Every morning he used to get up and sit on his knees with his head on the floor and hands by his head. I didn't know what he was doing until I went up and said, "dad what are you doing?" Dad – "I'm praying." Jesse - "But why, we aren't in church?" I knew what prayer was, since my aunt took us to our first church service, but I thought the only place you prayed was at church. When I was about five years old my aunt took my sister and all my cousins to a church in downtown Los Angeles. As we all took our seats my aunt looked over and said, "this is the house of God, so be on your best behavior." We listened to the sermon and then people began singing. People were standing up, jumping up and down, holding their hands up in the air, and singing at the top of their lungs. There was a lady in front of us and she was speaking really weirdly, and my cousins and I started mimicking her. "aba jaba, loo loo, coo coo" hahaha. My aunt reached over my cousins and grabbed me firmly and said "stop it this very moment, do not disrespect God! Bad things happen to those who disrespect God." Jesse – "Ok, I'm sorry Tia. I don't want God mad at me." As my dad finished praying, he said, "we can pray anywhere Jesse, whenever and wherever, God hears us. You just simply have to take the time to speak to Him.

God - The Punisher

I remember when I six, my sisters, brother, and some other kids from the neighborhood were playing soccer in the back yard of the apartments. I was sitting next to Karla; who I was madly in love with. As we were sitting there eating a bag of cheesy Cheetos, I caught a glimpse of my brother winding up his leg ready to kick the ball. I quickly grabbed Karla and pointed to my brother. My brother would always do this. He would always kick the ball as hard as he could, and it would go over the fence. One time it hit me in the face, and it was my fault! This time I was ahead of the game. I grabbed my dearly beloved and ducked. The ball went soaring over our heads and over the fence. He looked over at me and said, "Go get the ball. Jesse, you're the only one small enough to fit in-between the fence." I was the youngest in the family, so I was always chosen for things I didn't want to do. They all came over and pointed towards the fence, "go get it." Jesse - "Okay, okay, I'll go get it." I got up and handed the Cheetos over to Karla and told her I would be back. Now the fence was your classic black iron rods all across and about six feet tall with spears at the top. There were gaps in-between each rod, so I went towards the one that seems to have the biggest gap. I pressed my body against the rod, but I didn't fit. As everyone started laughing because I was too big to fit in-between the fence, I wondered, "maybe I shouldn't have eaten those Cheetos." I looked at the group and told them, "sorry I don't fit…" Right as I finished the sentence my brother says, "Jump the fence. Here I'll pick you up." He leads me towards the fence, picks me up, and helps me get to the top of the fence. I stand up there with one foot on a gap between a spear and the other foot on the other side of the spear. My heart races as my palms become sweaty. I look down and my legs feel glued to the fence. I look back and see everyone's lips moving but I can't hear anything. I close my eyes and tell myself "Jump. Take a step forward and jump." I held my breath as I leaned forward and jumped. I open my eyes and I was still in the air. "My shirt must be stuck to the fence", I thought. I wiggled up and down and boom I hit the ground. I walked towards the ball and picked it up with my left hand. As I turned around, I saw little blood drops on the ground that followed me all the way from the fence. I looked over to my right arm and saw a huge gash opened from the middle of my forearm going past my elbow. I quickly began to pray "God please don't let me die, don't punish me."

I woke up the next day with one hundred and sixty-six stiches. My arm was wrapped around in a white cloth, as I looked over and saw someone sleeping in the bed next to me. He had a white eye patch covering his left eye. I wondered what happened to him. Jesse - "Hi my name is Jesse." Little kid - "Hi, I'm Blake, why are you here?" I told him what happened and asked him the same question in return.

Little boy - "Well my mom and dad got into a huge argument. They were screaming at each other and my dad pulled out a gun to shoot my mom. I ran in between them to stop the fight as the gun went off and it hit me in the eye."

Jesse - "I'm sorry, are you ok?

Little boy - "Yeah, I'm ok, I just don't think I'll be able to see from this eye anymore.

I felt bad for him as I laid my head back down on my bed. The next day my mom came to visit and she took me to the cafeteria to eat. As we sat there, I asked her, Jesse - "Mom, how come God lets bad things happened, like to me and the little boy?" Mom - "Well Jesse, it's all part of Gods plan, God is in control. Just keep believing, it's all part of Gods plan." Jesse – "But I thought God punished bad people, did I do something bad?" Mom – "No Jesse, it's just Gods plan and He did this to you for a reason..." These words echoed throughout my life. "It's all part of Gods plan, he did this to you for a reason."

Not many months later passed the police came to our home and took me and all siblings away to the police station. One of my sisters was being abused by my moms' boyfriend. I did not know at the time; all I knew was that we were no longer allowed to live with my mom. My world was shattered and all I could think was, "what did I possibly do to make God this mad at me?" My dad at the time was living in New York working as a chef. My sister and I went into a foster home as my dad moved to LA to work on getting custody of us. After a year we finally moved into an apartment that was a couple of doors down from my aunt. I couldn't be happier for things to be back to normal, but in the back of my head, I was worried. I didn't understand why all these things happened. I couldn't think of a moment where I did something wrong that God would want to punish me this badly. All I hoped for was that nothing else bad would happen.

The big move

A few years flew by and my dad was having a hard time finding work. My uncle would call weekly telling my dad about all the work opportunities in Georgia and how much cheaper it was to live. After a year of saving up, my dad, my sister and I all moved to Georgia. I remember our apartment in Georgia like it was yesterday. You would walk in and immediately to your left would be the kitchen and the distinct smell of spicy peppers and shark oil. I don't know why, but my dad always made us drink shark oil. He said it would make us strong and give us a great immune system. I remember him giving me a spoon full of the shark oil as I held my nose shut with my index finger and thumb. I would start gag as I would ask my dad "what do I get if I do this." I would always get the same response, Dad - "a long life of course." Honestly it tasted like a fish had died two years ago and it shriveled up and someone squeezed all the liquid out of it and put it into my mouth. I quickly grabbed a lemon and squeezed it into my mouth so I wouldn't vomit. See growing up I was the vomit kid. I could never get into a car without vomiting five minutes into the ride. I remember my aunts' husband would take my cousins out for a car ride and my sister and I would always go with them. Of course, if the car ride was longer than five minutes I would vomit everywhere. One day my aunts' husband came as we were playing inside. I overheard his conversation with my aunt. Husband - "I want to take the kids out to Disneyland but I can't take Jesse and his sister. Especially Jesse, he vomits every time we're in the car." I felt awful. I knew it was a great inconvenience to take me anywhere in a car. My aunt quickly answered him Tia - "Well if you don't take Jesse and his sister then you can't take any of them." Husband - "But they're my kids, those other two aren't. Why can't I just take my kids, it doesn't make any sense." Tia – "They're all my kids. There is no difference between them so take all of them or take none!" He left the house storming angrily, and I quickly acted like I was playing with my cars. I knew my aunt loved me and I would miss her at times when we were in Georgia.

If you walked past the kitchen you would run into the dining table. I always wondered why we had this table because we really didn't eat at it very much. Most of the times we would eat at different times or my sister and I would eat, and my dad would eat after us. I very rarely remember my dad eating. If your turned to your right, you would be in the living room area now. This is where dad slept. There was a box spring, a blanket, a radio, and a pillow. I would ask my dad why his bed was a box spring and he always said that the hard box spring was better for his back, which I found funny because he never slept on it. I always saw him sleeping on the ground. Now between the dining room table and the living room there was a hallway that led to a bathroom. As you continued passed the bathroom, my room was to the right and my sisters room was to the left. My room was simple. I had a nice comfy bed in the furthest corner in the room and right across from it was a little stand with about a 12-inch T.V. I was so excited when we found this little T.V. It came with an antenna and it picked up most of the local channels. Now most of the good movies usually came on during the weekend. There was one movie in particular that I was super excited about and it was finally playing this Sunday. It was called "Saved the Last Dance." My sister and her friend were talking one day about how good it was, so I wanted to make sure I watched it. As you left my room, my sisters' room was to the right. She got the big room. She had the room with the bathroom all to herself. I wasn't really upset because I didn't mind sharing with dad. My dad and I were best friends. We played catch all the time, and at night when I would get scared, I would go and sleep next to him and he wouldn't say anything; he would simply give me some blanket to cover up with. The worst part was in the morning because he would always get up early. Even without an alarm clock. I don't know how he did it. It's as if he had some alarm in his head that just woke him up.

It was getting late one Saturday evening, and my sister came into my room to talk to me. She told me about how she had been sneaking out with her friends, and that I should make sure dad didn't find out. But I didn't want to do that, so I told her that I wanted to come too. I argued back and forth with her until I convinced her. She said "okay, come and sleep in my room because it's easier to sneak out." As we got ready for bed, I told dad that I was sleeping in my sisters room. About an hour later we slowly creaked the window open and push up enough to stick our heads out. We look out to see if my sisters' friends were there and as we took a glance to the right my heart dropped. My dad, very powerfully, asked "what are you doing? Do you think I am dumb? Close your window right now!" I look at my sister and said, "oh man you're in trouble." I ran to my room and closed the door. My dad came into the apartment and goes into my sisters' room to reprimanded her. He called me into her room so he could talk to me too, as he moved her large dresser in front of the window. Dad – "Now you can't sneak out. Goodnight" We all went to our beds and I start laughing as I laid on my bed just thinking about how stupid that was. Of course, dad was going to find out, I thought to myself. I slowly started to dose off as I heard a tap on my window. I lifted up the corner of the blinds and saw that it was one of my sisters' friends. I opened my window slightly where I can see everyone. There was a really pretty girl in the group that I actually like. They ask me where my sister was, and I told them the whole story and how my sister could not get out. They start to head off as I asked them where they were going. Kid 1 "To a hot tub in one of the neighborhoods down the street. You should come if you want." Jesse – "Me? Ya, ya, I'll come!" My heart raced as I put my shoes on as fast as I could and started heading towards my window. It was open enough that I could just pop off the screen and slowly start making my way out. Half of my body was out of the window and half still in my room, as I looked back at my door, I tried to listen for any creaks coming from inside the apartment. I could see a dim light from underneath the door, but that's always the kitchen light that stays on. I thought for a second "should I really do this? Dad really trusts me." I took my eyes away from the door and looked at my sisters' friends as they said, "are you coming or not?" I leaped the rest of my body out of the window. I closed my blinds, so it looked like my window was closed and I began running. I ran as lights became streaks in a runway, leading me towards the adventure. I could feel the nights' cold fly past me as my skin reacted with a quick shiver. I felt so free, I felt alive. We went to a pool that night and swam around and hung out for hours. The whole night was surrounded by laughter and friendship. It started to get really late, so we all went our separate ways and called it a night. As I walked back to our apartment, I thought about how much fun I had. I couldn't believe I just got to hang out with them. When I got closer to the apartment, I looked at my window and a cord of silence struck my whole body. I was paralyzed for a second. I had to get a closer look. I made my way over to my window and saw that it was closed. I pushed up and it was locked... "oh no, he knows." Dad must have woken up and checked in on me. I started panicking. I didn't want to knock on the front door. I didn't know what to do. So, I knocked on my sisters' window over and over and over until she finally woke up. "Dude who is this," she asked. "Dude I'm locked out, open the door" I said. Sister, "Alright." She opened the door. I tried my best to make the least sound possible as I ran to my room and shut the door behind me. Jesse - "At last, I'm in my bed. I feel safe." I start wondering what dad will say in the morning as I fell asleep.

I woke up late Sunday morning thinking "oh man I am in so much trouble." I knew my dad was going to be mad at me but worst of all, I knew that he was going to be disappointed in me. Jesse - "I should just stay in my room all day and hide. If I stay in here, then I can't get in trouble." Hours flew by until midafternoon, there was a knock on my door. "Okay Jesse this is it, just say sorry," I told myself. I opened my door. I saw my dad holding a beer as he asked, "are you hungry? I just made some lunch." I could smell the spiced chicken with onions, and peppers that he cooked. The food was calling me, but I felt so guilty and didn't want to confront him so I lied and said, "no I'm okay." Dad - "Okay," he said as he walked away. The day flew by as he left the house. Seconds turned into minutes and minutes turned into hours. It was getting late into the night. It was about eight and *Save the Last Dance* just started playing on T.V. I was so excited to finally watch it. I turned on the television as I quickly ran into the kitchen to grab all the food my hands could grab and continue hiding in my room. An hour went by and my sister and dad weren't home. I knew my sister was at her boyfriends and I knew my dad was probably at the bar across the street drinking. I knew he was upset with me so that's probably why he was drinking. I knew my dad would be mad if he came home and my sister wasn't home, so I left the apartment to go get her. I didn't want dad to be even more mad. As I walked out and started walking towards her boyfriend's house, I could see someone walking towards me. As our steps continued to bring us closer, I saw that it was my dad. I put my head down and kept walking towards him. As we met, I looked into his eyes and I could see the pain that I had caused him. In his breath, I could smell the magnitude of hurt being translated by his alcohol intake. He grabbed my shoulder and said, - "Jesse come back to the house, I want to talk to you." I shrugged my shoulder away and said, - "No Dad," and walked away. I don't know why I said no. It's not like I had an abusive father or something, he was a great father. I was just scared. I had never seen him that far gone with alcohol. I walked away and got my sister, as we made our way back to the apartment. When we got back, dad wasn't there so I guessed he went back to the bar. My sister went to bed, as she had to wake up earlier than me for school, and I went to my room and kept watching *Save the Last Dance*. I sat in my room as time went by, nine thirty, he's not home. Ten minutes, twenty minutes, thirty minutes, an hour goes by and he still isn't home. I start wondering if I should go to the bar and see if he's ok. Jesse - "Maybe I should go and check on him. No he's fine, you've felt like this before. He will be ok, just go to sleep, I told myself." I laid there waiting to hear his key unlock the front door. My eyes were began to grow heavier and heavier as sound came to be silent.

Suddenly, there was a loud banging coming from the door. Knock, knock, knock! I slowly pulled my covers off me, expecting someone else to get the door but then quickly wonder if that was dad and he just locked himself out. I jumped out of bed and headed toward the door. Knock, knock, knock! I looked through the peephole, and there stood two police officers/ I opened the door as they asked - "How old are you son." Jesse - "I'm,.. I'm,... I'm twelve, I mean thirteen." Officers - "Is there anyone else older in the house?" Jesse - "Yes, my sister." Officer - "How old is he?" Jesse - "She's, um, um sixteen." I ran to her room and woke her up, as the cops asked if they could come in. They ask us to take a seat at the dining room table. We sat down as we both looked at the cops wondering what was going on. Officers - "Your dad has been in an accident," Jesse - "Is he okay?" Sister - "What hospital is he at?" Jesse - "Can we go see him?" Officers - "He was hit by a car..." Jesse -"well, where is he, can we go see him?" Sister - "is he okay?" Officers - "I'm... I'm sorry but your father died instantly." My breath escaped as my mind looped those four words. "Your dad died instantly." Not my dad, not my dad, it can't be him, you have the wrong person. I tried to tell the cops they were wrong. No, no, no, no not my dad no that's not possible. Officers – "Here is his wallet with his ID card. That's how we knew to come to this apartment." Sister - "It's all your fault Jesse, you shouldn't have snuck out." I, I... no he can't be dead. No, no, no not him, not dad, not my dad, no, no, not dad not him, not dad! Officers -" We are so sorry your dad was crossing the street and got hit by a car." Tears streamed as my sister ran to her room. They asked us to pack a couple shirts, and shorts and told us to get into their car.

I lost my best friend that day. My father. My family. I had no home, no friends, no safety, no one to simply say I love you. I had nothing. Everything was taken away. I guess this was part of Gods plan.

Chapter 2 – Lost

The police officers put us in their car and drove us away. I looked out the window and wondered "what if I went back with him when he grabbed my shoulder?" "What if I never snuck out the night before?" "What if I apologized when he came knocking on my door during lunch time?" What

if.... What if it is my fault? What if I am the reason
he died? I couldn't help but wonder how different
this night could have been if I just something
diffrent... The cops dropped us off at a hospital and
they handed us over to child services. We were
assigned a social worker and she told us that
everything would be okay, and that we were going
to a nice home. She kept trying to comfort us, but I
couldn't hear anything, all I could hear was, what if?
Weeks and months passed by, jumping from group
home to foster home. I guess my sister got tired of it
because she ended up running away. I sat in tears
not knowing what to do. I would sit for dinner with
these families and see how they cared for their
children. I couldn't help but wish it was me inside
of the fairytale instead of watching it happen. I did
live with some strange families. I remember living
with this German family for a while and they loved
eating sausage. During one dinner, I sat back and
looked at them as they cut their sausage and dipped
it in mustard "Gross, I quickly said!" "Why
mustard?" Foster Parent - "Oh you don't understand

Jesse, this is German culture." He put another sausage on his son's plate and said, "here son, eat up so you can grow up to be strong." I also remember living with the Kilian's. They were such a great family. I remember coming downstairs one night and they were all playing board games and laughing. I stood by the stairs and just listened and wondered if I could join. I quickly thought "well I'll just grab some water and maybe they'll invite me to play." I went downstairs and reached for a glass and looked over and acted surprised Jesse - "Hh hi, that looks fun" they respond Foster Family " oh yaaaa…" and they continued to play. My water finished filling up as I said, "well good night, I guess." Foster Family - "Goodnight." I went back up to my room, sat the glass full of water on the nightstand and laid down. I turned over to the wall as I wrapped the covers over my head. The warm wall gave me comfort and felt as if I had someone there for me. I starred at the wall as I wondered if I would ever have my dad back, or at least my sister. I kept staring as tears ran down my face. Tears of confusion, anger, pain, and loneliness. I've never felt so alone in my life. Some days I would just stare out the window thinking somehow my dad would walk by because he was coming to get me. I hoped, but he never came.

Group home

One of the hardest parts was going back to school. I would sit at my desk with my head down so no one could see the tears I was trying to hold off. People would come up and say, "I'm so sorry Jesse, I heard what happened, Mr. Sharp told us." I would quickly respond, Jesse - "I don't know what you are talking about everything is fine," and storm off. Each time someone would bring up what happened I quickly denied it. I tried my best to convince people that it wasn't true. I tried my best to convince myself that it wasn't true. I quickly became short with teachers and tried anything to pull away attention from my dad's death. I started stealing and getting into fights to the point that my school had no choice but to expel me. My foster parents ended up asking me to leave, and the social worker took me to a group home. As she dropped me off, she said, Social worker - " I know you are angry Jesse, but this world will only become uglier if you keep fighting it. If you aren't happy just fake it, if you are angry act happy, if you can't smile, just make yourself. This is your last stop, I don't know where else you could live if you get kicked out of this group home, so try your best." I looked over to her and asked Jesse – "Are you sure this is it? It looked like an office building." Social worker – "Yes, this is your last chance." When you first walked in, there was a glass office and someone sitting behind the desk. As I walked toward the office door, I could see a long hallway with kids coming in and out the doors on both sides of the hallway. I sat in the office and the social worker said, "Welcome home." I met the group home parent, and he showed me to my room. As you walked into the room there were two bunk beds, two dressers, and that was pretty much the room. The beds had a little blanket with the pillow at the head. It was like I was in a military movie and these were our bunks. I dropped my bags on the floor and laid back on the bed. I looked up and saw five wooden boards holding up the top bed. I turned over and ran my fingers across the white wall. Jesse - "Just me, and you again huh?" The door opened and three guys came in Guys - "Hey you must be the new guy, I'm Tony." Jesse - "Hi I'm Jesse." Guys - "I'm Alex, I'm Derrick." Jesse - "Well this place seems fun." Tony - "yeah it's okay, just be careful with who you're around." We all headed to lunch as I turned the corner, I ran right into one of the foster kids. Jesse -"So sorry man, I didn't even see you." Foster Kid- "yo watch yo self-man you goin get hurt" Jesse - "Sorry it was an accident." Foster Kid- "better be." I kept walking toward the cafeteria as people kept giving me funny looks. I looked around and I saw some kids with bandanas in their back pocket. I remember seeing bandanas in L.A. like that, but they were gold in L.A. Here they were blue and some red ones. I knew that they had to be gang related, so I quickly looked to find my roommates and sat down with them. Jesse -"Hey so are people in gangs in here?" Tony - "ya sorta, they're either in, or just repping it. I rep the bloods cuz then I know people got my back no matter what." Jesse - "Is it that bad in here?" Tony - "It can be." I looked down at my food as I wondered how long I would have to live here. Jesse - "I can't be bad, I'll probably get killed and even if I did get kicked out, where am I going to go next?" That night I went back to my room to think about the day and what I could do. I needed a way out. Dark grew quickly as I heard the foster parent yell out, "let's go everyone lights out," my roommate came in and quickly got into his bed and shut off the lights. Tony - "so Garcia, what's your story?" Jesse - "uh, what do you mean?" Tony- "Why you here? Where's your family?" Jesse - "uh, I don't know, I just don't have one, but uh, what about you?" I quickly flipped it to him so I wouldn't have to go into detail about my past. Tony - " Well you know my mama is a big dope head, selling and stuff and here I am." Jesse - "oh wow I'm sorry...

How long have you been here?" Tony - "this will be my second year." As he finished his sentence the door started to wiggle around. "Who there?" Tony quickly shouted out. The door suddenly busted open and seven guys walked in and shut the door behind them. "Shut up Tony," one of them said. "So, what's up new kid, I saw you were wearing a blue shirt today so you down with the Crips?" Jesse - "Uh nah man nah it was just a shirt, you can have it though if you want." They grew closer to my bed as I quickly got up and leaned against the bunkbed. "So, what you repping fool?" as one of the kids got close to me and pushed me against the wall. Jesse - "I don't know man, I don't know" The pressure grew as he held me against the wall. I pushed his hads off as I threw up a gang symbol I saw once. Foster kid - "Well oh shit, you know what this means right?" "You in our house and for doing that shit we gotta all punch you in the chest five times" Jesse - " but I, I, I…" Foster kid - "There ain't no buts, Ricky come hold this fool." They held me down as they all swung and hit me in the chest over and over and over again. I gasped for air as they walked out of the room. Foster kids - "You better not throw that back up again, cuz next time, we won't stop." I laid on the concrete floor as I looked up to Tony stretching out his hand towards me. He began to laugh as he said - "You should have said Bloods, bro!"

I laid in silence that night as I tried to hold my tears back. I closed my eyes and prayed,

> "God... I don't know what I did to make you so angry at me but I'm sorry... Everyone keeps telling me you have a plan and good things are coming but I can't help feeling hopeless and lost. God I miss my dad, I miss the days we would throw the ball around, I miss seeing him look outside during a thunderstorm, I miss him picking me up at the school bus stop with an umbrella when it was pouring rain outside, I miss him saying goodnight to me. Lord I miss my family. I

know I shouldn't have snuck out and I shouldn't have said I was in a gang but God please get me out of here. Please get me out of this place and let me go back to a foster home. God please help me. I promise to do good in school, and whoever I live with, I will treat them with respect. God please.

Months went by. I stared at the same wall every night, wondering if I would ever have a home. Summer was ending and everyone started going to school registration. I couldn't believe that it was almost five months since I first got here. My social worker dropped by after registration and told me I was going to spend the rest of the day with her. When I got into the car, I saw two book bags and I quickly asked her, "what are those for?" Social Worker - "Oh, those are for you, we provide you with everything you need for school." Jesse -"But why two bags" Social worker - "So if you run out you'll have an extra one." I liked my social worker. She was always there trying to give me advice. She knew I hated where I was living but she couldn't do anything about it, she didn't have anywhere else to take me. As we drove to a local restaurant, I asked her, Jesse - "do you think we can stop by the first foster home I lived in? It's by the restaurant." Social worker- "Uh sure... but why do you want to go there." I couldn't tell her the real reason I wanted to go there so I said, Jesse - "well I grew really close to the other kids there and I know they could use this extra book bag." Social worker - "Wow that's really nice of you, sure we'll stop by for a couple minutes." See the real reason I wanted to stop by is my sister ran away from this foster home and I knew she went to her boyfriend's house after running away and he lived down the street. I wanted to give this book bag to the foster mom so she could give it to my sister. As we got close to the house, I told my case worker, Jesse - "hey I'll just knock on the door and drop it off so we can go quickly." Social worker - "Yeah that's fine Jesse." When she stopped the car, I bolted out with the book bag, and went straight to the door. I knocked a couple of time

as I looked around hoping they were home. The
foster parent opened the door with a confused
expression on her face. Jesse - "Hey," I said, "sorry
to stop by like this, I just wanted to drop by and
leave this book bag here. I don't know if you see my
sister much, but I wanted to drop it off so if you
ever see her, she could have it for school." Foster
Parent - "Of course Jesse, that's really sweet of
you." "Where are you living now?" Jesse -"I'm in a
group home south of the city..." Then I explained
everything that had happened to me. Foster Parent -
"Jesse that's horrible, well you seem to have
changed some. If you promise to try and be better
you can come back here, it might be better than
where you are now. I'll call your social worker and
get it set up." Jesse - "Seriously?!" "That would be
great, and I promise I will be good, keep my head
down, and focus on school." Foster Parent - "Of
course Jesse, I'll see you soon." I ran back to my
social worker and told her about everything that
happened, and her face lit up as bright as mine.
Social worker - "That's great Jesse, now remember

what I told you even if you don't feel like life is fair just fake it, just put on a smile no matter what, and just be strong."

That week I moved all my things back into the foster home and registered to the school I was once kicked out of. I knew I had one shot left, but that is all I needed.

I was now in eighth grade and it seemed that everyone had forgotten that I got kicked out and my father had died. Whenever I walked to classes, I kept my head down and also made sure not to talk. The assistant principal brought me into his office for a pep talk. "Jesse this is a new year for you, what happened last year happened in the past, so let's just focus on this year, and if you ever need me just ask." Jesse - "of course, thank you, and if you ever need any help let me know." Assistant Principal -"Okay, Jesse thank you." Most of my days were going to school, studying, and sleeping. I was so behind compared to everyone else. I would stay after school some days to get extra help and walk back to my foster parents house. Days grew into weeks and weeks grew into months. One day while I was sitting in class, a student aid came into the classroom and said the assistant principal wanted to see me. My heart grew silent, as I've heard those words many times before. I wondered as I got out of my desk, "why he wanted to see me?" I knew I hadn't done anything wrong, but I couldn't help but feel guilty. As I walked towards his office I started coming up with apologies. I opened his door and he asked me to take a seat. "Jesse do you know why I called you in today?" Jesse - "uh, no clue." Assistant Principal - "Well I need your help." Jesse -"help on what?" Assistant Principal - "Well there are these gang symbols in the bathroom, and I took some pictures of them and wanted to see if you knew what they were." Jesse - "Oh, sure!" We sat there for an hour talking about different gangs, what they mean, and all of their different colors. Assistant Principal - "Wow Jesse you've really helped me a lot today." Jesse - "Of course, well I better get going." Assistant Principal - "Jesse one last thing before you leave." Jesse - "What's up." Assistant Principal - "Since you've been so good this year we have nominated you for an award called *The Most Improve Student Award*, and you will have a chance to go to the *Omni* Hotel in Atlanta for a nice lunch with the principal of the whole school. Jesse - "Wow no way!" Assistant Principal - "Yes way. So, make sure you wear something nice next Monday." Jesse - "I can't believe it, thank you so much." Assistant Principal- "You deserve it," he said as I headed back to class. I couldn't believe that out of all the students in the school I was the one that they picked. I guess my social worker was right, you just have to put on a smile even if you have to fake it.

The week flew by as thoughts of the award ceremony consumed my mind. It was late Sunday night and I laid there in my bed thinking about who I would meet, what type of food there would be, and how I would look walking across the stage. I turned on my side and closed my eyes. Minutes passed and I turned over to the other side. I began to think of school math problems "c'mon just think of your teacher teaching," I told myself. I kept tossing and turning and couldn't find a single comfortable position on my bed. I got up and went to the bathroom and looked for the Vicks. I opened the container on my way back to bed, and I lifted the Vicks up to my nose and inhaled deeply. The aroma quickly traveled to my brain as it sparked a memory. When I was little, there was nights when I couldn't sleep and I would get out of bed and tiptoe over to my dad's bed and say, "Dad.... Dad... I can't sleep." Dad - "What's wrong son?" Jesse - "I don't know, I just can't sleep." Dad - "It's okay. Come here. Let's go back to bed." He would walk me back to my bed and as I laid down, he would get the Vicks. He would get a little bit and rub it on my chest and tell me stories until I fell asleep. Before he left, he would bend down and kiss my forehead and say, "I love you son." I looked at the Vicks as I stood in the hallway and rubbed a little on my chest and said, "I hope I make you proud one day Dad."

The next morning, I woke up early and made sure to iron my clothes and get to the bus stop early. I did not want to miss today. When I got to school, I went to the principal's office and we headed downtown to the Omni Hotel. As we drove down through the crazy traffic of Atlanta, she began asking me questions, "So what changed this year from last year?" Jesse - "Well I learned quickly that being upset at the world and taking it out on people doesn't get you far in life. I've lived in some awful places and I'm okay with acting happy if that means I can live somewhere safe." We kept driving as she kept asking me questions about my experiences at the group home. When we got to the hotel, I looked up and stood in awe as I have never seen a ceiling so high. You could see glass elevators rising and descending and all I could do was stand there in awe. The room was beautiful. It was filled with lights. There were white tablecloths, and more silverware, plates and cups than I've ever seen before. I only needed one fork. I didn't know why they put down more. We sat down at our table, as someone came across the stage welcoming everyone and telling us to enjoy our meals. We began to eat, and my principal asked, "So Jesse why are you so mad at the world?" Jesse - "oh, I don't know." I knew exactly why I just didn't want to talk about it. Principal - "Well there has to be a reason," she said while she looked up into my eyes, "Won't you tell me?" Jesse - "Um well I've been mad because my Dad died, and my sister ran away and now I have no family." I couldn't believe those words came out of my mouth. How can Dad be dead? I quickly looked down and tried to hold back tears. Principal - "I'm so sorry Jesse. I had no idea. You know my husband and I are thinking about being foster parents and adopting. You said that you would like to have somewhere safe to live? Jesse - "Yeah, that would be good." Inside my head I was thinking, Me? live with the principal? No way, she doesn't want a kid like me. I think she's just saying all of this because she feels bad for me. Principal - "Well I'll look into it." That night I laid in my bed and looked out the window. "God, I know we haven't talked in a while, and I know you might be mad at me for the things that I've done, but I pray for a better future. I pray for a better home." I couldn't help but dream about how great it would be to live with my principal and her husband. I would be their only child and it would be a family again. I quickly shook my head "be real and don't get your hopes up." I told myself. I turned my pillow over to the cool side and told myself, "I know but I can dream."

Chapter 3 - Hope

I remember it like it was yesterday. My new foster parents called me early in the morning letting me know they would be picking me up during lunch. I jumped out of my bed as my heart started to pump faster. "I'm going to be living with my principal and her husband?" "No way, this can't be true!" I ran to the kitchen and grabbed a couple of trash bags and started to throw everything I owned in the bags. I had to make sure my clothes were in there, oh, and my shoes. I looked around. All that was left was my book bag. I put my bags by the front door and looked at the room one last time. I couldn't believe I was finally going to live in a good home with people that actually cared about me and wanted to be a family. Jesse - "Maybe this empty and lonely feeling will finally go away with my new family. I looked at the white wall, as I said "goodbye, my friend." I was so excited that I stood outside and waited for them to come. As noon struck, their car came rolling down the hill as doubt crept into my mind. "What if they don't like me? What if they want to get rid of me after a year? You have to be good; you have to be respectful, and you have to put a smile on your face, this is my last chance." I couldn't imagine having to go back to the places I've been. They got out of their car and told me to put my things in. The drive to their house was about 30 minutes. The streets were surrounded by trees that had low hanging branches. As we turned into their neighborhood, every house seemed to be the same. We drove up a driveway and they said, "Welcome home Jesse." I didn't know how to respond so I quickly laughed and got out of the car to get my bags. They led me to my room and showed me my closet, desk, and T.V. I couldn't have been more excited. Foster parents - "Well take some time and unpack, we'll start dinner," Jesse - "Okay, sounds great." As the door closed behind me, I exhaled deeply. I didn't know why, but I was nervous. I wasn't sure what it would be like to live with them yet, whether we would get along or if they even wanted to keep me for long. I've lived in so many places that I knew I just had to say as little as possible and make sure I stayed out of their way. If they didn't notice me maybe they wouldn't want to get rid of me. As I headed downstairs, all the dogs began to bark. "Brogan, Nula, shhhhhh…" my foster mom quickly yelled out. "I'm sorry, I quickly said, "I didn't mean to scare them." Foster Mon - "Oh no it's okay, sit down dinner is ready." I sat down and we began to pray. Wow, they must be Christian, I thought. I was hungry and dove straight into my meal. It became silent so I thought I should say something. "So, are you guys Protestants? I asked." Foster mom - "No, we're both Catholic. We've been Catholic ever since we were little. I also forgot to mention that living with us means you have to go to Church with us." Jesse - "Oh no worries that's okay." Foster Mom - "Jesse living here means you will have rules and expectations to live by, and that we expect you to respect that, but of course we will also have fun. We signed you up for football summer work-outs and we will get you signed up to our Church so that you can receive the Sacraments." Jesse - "Okay, that all sounds great." I really wasn't listening to what they were saying. The lasagna that was in front of me was the best meal I've ever had in my life. All I could think about was finishing it all to make sure that no one would try to take it away. When everyone else finished, I got up and took their plates and washed them. "Thank you so much," they both said." We headed downstairs to watch T.V. An hour went by and I started to get bored. I was pretty tired, so I told them I was heading to bed. As I got up, they both said "oh we will walk you up." Jesse - "Uh okay," I said not sure what else to say. We walked upstairs as I thanked them for such a wonderful day and the lasagna. "Of course," they said, "we will make it more in the future." Foster parents - "Well goodnight Jesse, we love you." Jesse - "Uh... ok... goodnight," I stuttered and ran up the steps. Uh ok goodnight, what kind of response was that, I thought to myself. I love you, they said they loved me, but they just met me. How could my foster parents love me already? I've never had a foster parent say they loved me. Maybe they really do want to keep me. Shoot why didn't I say it back? Are they going to be mad at me because I didn't say I love you back? My mind raced as I laid in my bed wondering if this was it, if I screwed up already and they were going to ask me to leave tomorrow. I looked up at the ceiling, and said, they love me, but how? I turned over and pulled the sheets up to my shoulders. Maybe tomorrow they won't say, I love you, maybe it just slipped out.

The game of inches

Summer workouts kicked off in early July. I didn't have many shirts, so I threw on a shirt that said, "Chick Magnet" and a pair of athletic shorts. Now at this point, I probably weighed close to 300 pounds. Needless to say, I was pretty chunky. When we got to the school, there was about one hundred people on the field, which made me smile because then maybe I could hide in the crowd. I got out of the car, told my foster mom bye, and headed toward the field. As I walked to the gates people looked over and said, "Chick Magnet, yeah right fat boy." "Guys look at this guy's shirt." Jesse – "Uh oh," "maybe I shouldn't have worn this shirt." A whistle blew and the coached yelled, "okay everyone get in one straight line on the end zone." We walked towards the end zone. Everyone was pushing to fit inside the edges of the line. Coach - "Now when I blow my whistle you will run all the way down to the other end zone and make it back here in eighteen seconds." I look over as everyone begins to chatter, "what? How many times do you think we will have to run this?" I asked. Kid 1 - "I don't know but you better make it Chick magnet." I couldn't let them down. I didn't want to be the one kid that didn't make it. I dug my right foot into the line and looked straight down the field." "Eighteen seconds," I told myself, "I can do this." The whistle blew and we took off. Stride after stride I looked to make sure no one else is behind me. Coach - "eight, seven, six, five..." the coach started counting down as I am still on the fifty-yard line. I push forward. ", four, three, two.." I leap forward and crossed the line. I made it! I bent over and latched my hands on my knees. I made it. "Good job guys," the coach yells, "now just fourteen more." Jesse - "What?" "14 more, there's no way I'm going to make it." The whistle blew again, before I could get over the fact that we had to run fourteen more. I took off seconds behind the larger part of the crowd. I pushed my legs and kept looking down toward the other end zone as I heard our coach counting down. "I'm not going to make it," I thought as I looked around. A couple guy's yelled out, "come on Chick magnet! You can do it! Push!" I leaned forward and pushed as hard as I could and made it in the last second. Jesse - "Wow," "I'm not going to make 13 more, I know that much." I looked around again as everyone tried to catch their breath. The whistle blew again. I was caught off guard, and started late again, by the time I was at the 50-yard line the coach already started counting down from four seconds. I knew this time I wasn't going to make it, but I still wanted to give it my best. "Four, three…" "come on Chick Magnet, make it to the line," "Two, one." I was still barely at the twenty-yard line, as myself and a couple other people didn't make it on time. Coach - "Now we had a couple people not make the time, so that one will not count, and you all have to run it again." Eyes glared at me, and people began yelling, "come on people," I felt awful, because I knew I was letting everyone down. The whistle blew again, so I took off as hard as I could. Over and over for the next twenty runs myself and a couple of other people didn't make it. The coach blew his whistle and told us to meet him at the fifty yard-line. Coach - "Good job everyone. This was a good day for your first workouts. Now there were a few of you that couldn't make the time so make sure you are building your endurance. We are running these all summer long so make sure you are ready. Good work everyone. I'll see you all tomorrow." "Lions on three. One, two, three. LIONS!" I got up, and my legs felt like jelly. I headed towards the car and wondered how I was going to make it this whole summer. I can't let the team down again. I have to make sure I push myself. When I got home, I asked if I could join a gym and start working out more. Days turned into weeks and weeks turned into months. My relationship with my foster parents grew. They continued to say they loved me, but I could never say it back. I couldn't make myself say mom and dad. The word dad felt like gravity tugging on my throat and heart. I want to love them, but I just don't know how to. Late at night I would wonder where my sister was, and if I would ever see her again. I wondered how my other siblings and my cousins were doing. I felt so lucky that I had a family now, but I still felt so alone. I missed running up to my dad and him smiling at me. I missed him telling me stories about how when I was little, I would get a raw hotdog, and stick it in peanut butter, and run around the house without my diaper. I miss the safety that came with simply being with him. The world used to feel so small, but now I felt stranded in the vastness of the roaring sea.

My freshman and sophomore year flew by. I was finally good at football and all my hard work was paying off. Now I was headed towards my junior year and college coaches started sending me letters wishing me a good season and that they would be watching.

Shiloh vs PRHS - 2007

My elbows were pressed against my quads as I leaned forward with closed eyes thinking about the first game of my junior season. I remember all the hot summer days, all the sweat, all the tears, and all the bumps and bruises. This is the day; I have to show up so I can get a scholarship to school. Coach- "It's about that time, let's go!" I stood up like a soldier ready for battle. We headed down to the field as we could hear the crowd roaring. It was the first game of the season and people expected a state championship by the end of the year. We stood behind the banner at the closest endzone. The sky was filled with heavy clouds and a couple of raindrops began to fall. Team Captain - "We have worked too hard, too long, to not win this game. Let's go out there and show everyone what we are really made of. Let's go out there and make a sound that lets everyone know it's going to be a long season for them. Let's win this game! Lions on three, one, two, three, Lions!" We ran through the banner and headed to our endzone. Coach- "This is a good team so don't think that this will be a cake walk. Now it will probably start raining here soon so we will be running the ball most of time and sneaking in some passes, so keep your feet moving and let's get this wim." We won the coin toss and elected to receive. We huddled up the offense and went over the first couple of plays. I was playing offensive guard and, some defense, but I seemed to have mastered the position of offensive guard. We ran out to the field to run our first play. I could feel the rain dripping off of my pants as I moved to put my hand on the ground. There was someone lined up right in between myself and the center, and I knew I had to get the middle linebacker but I needed to help the center too. The ball hiked. The center and I pushed the defender back. I could feel the center start to take control of the defender. I saw the middle linebacker stepping up, so I let go of the first defender and ran towards the middle linebacker. I exploded off the ground and hit the middle linebacker right in the chest until he was on the floor. Jesse - "It's going to be a long game baby, so get ready." A couple of plays later, we scored our first touchdown, and heading in a great direction for our first game. My blocks were perfect, and I could feel all of the summer practices paying off. The rain kept falling and my cleats and socks began to weigh me down. Areas on field began to form puddles. We all looked at each other and said, "Ya! This is our type of football!" Coach - "The rain is starting to really come down so we are going to keep running the ball. Lineman make your blocks and we will win this game!" We ran back out to the field as the sky grew darker and darker. We were running a power play and the defender was lined up right in between the center and myself. I looked over to the center and gave him a smile because I knew we were going to pancake this kid. The ball hiked, and the defender pushed hard to split in between myself and the center. I pushed my hand toward the middle of his shoulder pads, but my hand slipped. The center went full force trying to push him out of the way, as the linebacker began to come up. The defender slipped to the ground and landed on my foot. I couldn't move my leg as the middle linebacker got closer and closer. Jesse - "I've got to move my leg," I thought, "but it's stuck, it's stuck!" The middle linebacker comes in full speed to make the tackle. As he hits me, I started to fall with him into the running back, but my leg was still stuck, and it began to bend sideways. I screamed "my leg, my leg, it's going to break!" I fell on the ground as I hear my leg snap towards the opposite side. I laid there and screamed out, "my leg, my leg, it's broken!" I laid there staring at the dark sky as it continues to pour. I ripped my helmet off, and yelled, "why God, why do you keep punishing me!? Just leave me alone. I want nothing to do with you! All you do is bring pain and sorrow to my life." All I could think about was all of the hot summer days, the late nights at the gym, and all of the work that I put into finally being in a good place in my life, and then it's gone, all over again. Jesse - "God why do you hate me? I want nothing to do with you." My coach ran onto the field with the medics. Jesse - "Coach is it bad?" Coach - "I'm sorry son. I'm so sorry." The cart came down onto the field to pick me up and put me in the back of an ambulance. My mind began to race wondering if I would ever play again. The doctor looked at my leg and said, "Jesse you aren't getting any blood to your toes. We need to pop this back into place now, so you don't lose your foot." He grabbed my leg and pushed as hard as he could until my leg popped back into place.

That night I laid in the hospital bed staring at the
ceiling as tears streamed down my face. Jesse -
"What have I done to deserve such a life? What
have I done to make God so angry with me? All my
scholarships all my hopes are gone in the matter of
seconds. All that hard work, and for what?" I
couldn't help but miss my dad. I wondered what he
would say to me or how he would comfort me. I
wondered if he would have still been proud. The
nurse came in to give me pain medicine. "Here take
this and try to get some sleep," she said. "The
doctor will be in in the morning to speak to you
about surgery."

The next morning the doctor came in with the scans
of my leg to let me know that I've basically
dislocated my knee, torn every single ligament, and
some muscles. Jesse - "I hear ya doc, but can I play
again? Can I play football again?" Doctor - "I don't
think you understand this type of injury is one we
rarely see in football. Your injury looks like you
were in a bad car accident." He looked at me, and

with a shaky voice said, "I just don't know if you will ever be able to play again. I'm sorry." Jesse - "No doc, I'm sorry, because I am going to do whatever it takes to play again."

A week later I had surgery and it went well. Throughout the healing process all I could think of was being back in the field. All I've come to learn was the field and working out, but now I couldn't do any of it. Months flew by and my recovery process kept taking longer and longer as I started to strengthen my leg. Friends would come by and try to comfort me by taking me to church or asking me to come to youth group, but I just didn't see the point of it anymore. If people go to church for hope and pray for good things but only bad things happen, why keep going? Why would I pray to someone that has only brought pain and sorrow to my life? It was pointless. People even tried to say that it's God's plan. Well if God planned this for me, then he must hate me. I started walking and finally was able to run, but all I could think about was the voice that kept saying, "you can't play football ever again." I pushed myself every day in the gym. I pushed harder than ever before and was able to play in my senior year of high school. I wasn't as strong and I could feel how much weaker I was, as I struggled to block at times, but I was playing. My senior year came and went. I had the opportunity to play football at a small local college and took it immediately. I wanted to make a statement and make it loud and clear. My relationship with my foster parents grew distant. I grew further and further away from them, because I couldn't imagine getting close to someone and losing them again. I just wanted to be left alone. I felt like a cursed child, and that all I could ever offer was a burden. While hope was in the air, it quickly left me with broken and empty.

Chapter 4 - Two Weeks

My dorm room was perfectly symmetrical. On both
sides of the rooms there was, two windows, two
beds, two desks, two drawers, and two closets. I
looked at both sides as I tried to judge which side
was best. There was no distinctions or marks that
would make one side better than the other, so I
chose the one on the right. I unpacked my bags and
jumped onto my bed. I looked around the room. The
big white walls left the room feeling empty. I
needed to put some posters up or maybe bring a tv

with me next time I was home. The room seemed so quiet, so I played some music to draw out the emptiness. I laid there as the music played wondering if I would make friends at college and if football would go well. I couldn't help but think of what the point of all of this was. I'm was not as good I used to be, what's the point of even playing? What is my point? Why has this world been so cruel to me? I just wish dad was here to tell me what I should do or at least guide me. I wonder what he would say. I turned over to face the wall and ran my fingers through the brick cracks, and wondered what life would be like if dad and my sister and myself were all still together.

The next morning, I woke up to a snoring sound and quickly looked over to the next bed. Who is that? I wondered. I looked around and saw his football cleats and gear. Jesse – "Oh, it must be my roommate. What time is it? I must have been really tired." I looked at the clock and it was 4:30 a.m., and we had to be at practice at 5. I jumped out of bed and turned on the lights. "Hey man," I said out loud "we gotta go, we have practice." Roommate - "Alright man, thanks for waking me up. I'm Robert by the way." Jesse - "Cool man, I'm Jesse."

My eyes were heavy as I put my helmet on. Coach yelled, "line up!" I've heard this before. I knew we were about to run, but I didn't have the same motivation as I did as when I was younger. Why was I putting myself through the same torture? Why should I run? Why should I bleed and sweat? There's no point anymore. I've tried so hard and at the end it's the same story. The whistle blew and we all sprinted. Whistle after whistle. Why? Consumed my thoughts, but I had no answer.

Weeks flew by as my thoughts grew deeper and emptier at the same time. Hate ran through my blood as I tried to find answers to the lingering questions. Nights were covered with tears as I asked more and more, what is the point? I didn't want to feel any more, I just wanted to be numb. Numb to the reality of my pain and numb to the reality of my emptiness. I quit football and began drinking a lot and smoking. I did anything and everything to simply fill that emptiness. My dorm room became the party room. We filled our room with friends and played beer pong all day. Days became weeks and weeks became months and we kept drinking and smoking. Sundays were always the best days. We always started drinking so early, because games would come on T.V. at 1pm. "Hey instead of beer pong, let's play Liquor pong," I told everyone. "Hell ya, let's go!" I grabbed a handle of Liquor and some mixers and poured them all together. We started playing and people came and went. My roommate and I were crushing it. We were beating everyone that tried to play against us. "Shots for everyone!" someone shouted. We began taking shot after shot after shot and time began to slip away. I saw myself eating and laughing as we ran around campus. I could hear everyone talking but it was as if I was on autopilot, and I was simply watching.

Night came quickly, and I remember sitting in the back of a car telling myself, "I'm just going to take a little nap right here…"

"Beep, beep, beep…" My eyes were still closed when I heard a faint sound, "beep, beep, beep." I opened my eyes slowly, as the light blinded my vision for the first couple of seconds. I lifted my arm to stretch, but it quickly jolted back. I could feel a steel band keeping it from moving. My eyes adjusted, and I realized I was in a hospital, but why, what happened? I looked down at my hand and it was handcuffed to the steel bar of my bed? What the hell is going on? Why am I handcuffed. I looked around for a nurse. I saw a police officer standing right outside the door. Shit, I yelled to myself, I hope they didn't find my fake ID. I reached over to my pockets with my left hand to try to find it. Phew, I exhaled. It was still in my pocket. I saw the nurse coming my way. She turned to grab the attention of the police officer as she walked into my room. Nurse - " How are you feeling. Jesse – "I'm feeling ok... but what happened?" Nurse – "Well son you had a little too much to drink and... well... I'll let the police officer explain the rest." Cop – "How are you feeling son?" Jesse – "uh, I'm ok but what happened?" Cop – "We'll cover all that later, let's make sure you're okay first." The nurse checked my vitals and told the cop right outside the door, "he's good to go when you're ready to take him." The cop came in and said, "so you've two options; I can either handcuff you and walk you out or you can be cooperative and walk with me to the police station." Jesse - "Yeah, uh, I'll just walk, but why do I have to go to the police station?" The cop unlocked the handcuffs, and we began walking me to his car. Cop – "Well son we came and arrested you last night, because we got a complaint of you breaking into cars. Three people claimed that you had tried breaking into their cars, and that you fell asleep in one." Jesse – "So what does that mean for me? I didn't hurt anyone. I was drunk and I was probably just trying to go to sleep." Cop – "Son, each car you broke into is a felony. So, you have three felonies and you'll have to fight it in court, which will be about three months from now. Do you understand?" My heart sank at his words... "but, but I have to stay here until my court date?" By this point we made it to the police station. Cop - "Yes, unless you can get someone to come bail you out, but each felony holds a 5,000 bond so they'll have to pay that prices times three...." I held back tears as we entered the jail. They began to process me. They took my pictures and held me in a processing cell. Three months? What about school? What will people think? I bit my teeth down as my eyes began to swell. My mind raced as I held one of the bars with my right hand and looked out, God what did I ever do? A cop came around and yells, "Garcia you get your one call, are you ready?" Jesse - "Ya." He brought me out and I began thinking, what am I going to say? My foster parents are going to freak out. What if they don't come get me? We got to the phone and I began to dial my foster parents number. With each ring, my thoughts crisscrossed from hoping they didn't pick up, to hoping they do.

"Please leave a message for...." they didn't pick up. I put the phone back down and looked up at the officer and said, "they didn't pick up, but can I try again in thirty minutes?" Cop - "Yes, we'll take you back to the cell and you can try again soon." I passed through the processing cell and thought about what I would say. I've let everyone down. I'm such a failure. I couldn't think of how I got here. Thirty minutes passed until the officer came back around and said, "Okay let's try this again." I dialed their number again and it began to ring. Silence covered me as the ring drew out longer and longer. "Hello?!...." Jesse - "Uh, oh hey, it's Jesse." Foster Dad - "Hey what's going on?" Jesse - "Um, I'm sorry, I don't know how to say this, but I'm in jail." I bit my teeth harder as I could hear the disappointment in his voice, Foster dad - "what did you do?" I could barely speak as the words I rushed out, "I don't really know, but here's the officer." I handed the phone to the officer as he explained my fate to my foster father on the phone. The officer hung up the phone and I looked up and asked, "well what did he say?" Cop - "They are on their way." I wish I could say I felt relived, but at this point I didn't even know if they would be able to help me.

Hours went by until the officer came by and said, "your parents want to talk to you." They sat me down behind a see-through glass. My foster parents came around the corner as I caught their eyes, and I couldn't hold it together anymore. I couldn't stay strong anymore, and the sea of tears poured out as they put their hands up to the glass and reassured me they would get me out. All I could muster to say was, "I'm so sorry, I'm so sorry." I could hear them raising their voices at the cops to figure out what the best way to get me out. I sat in that chair covered in tears and wondered why my life was filled with so much pain. The officer came and got me and said, "your parents have paid your bond, you're free to go." I headed towards the front door and met them with hugs and tears. We walked outside and there was a man there waiting to talk to my parents. I didn't know who he was, but he kept saying, "you're not a criminal, you're not a criminal, and everything will be okay." We got into the car, and my foster parents started to speak to each other about getting a lawyer and how they were going to fight this. I just didn't know what to say. I was still lost. We stopped to get food, then they took me back to my dorm. We sat there, and they told me, "before we leave you need to make sure that you don't do anything else. No drinking. No nothing, just school. We'll figure this whole thing out, just don't worry about it. They left. I closed the door behind them and collapsed on the ground. Jesse – "Why God, why must you hate me?" Why must you put me through all of this, for what? ... what have I ever done..." I've got up with rage and threw all my books on the floor, "why God?" I threw my chair across the room. "God answer me, answer me right now." "Why do you hate me so much?" Answer me! I fell to my knees beside my bed. "God why?" "What have I ever done." "You've taken everything from me. I can't keep pretending I'm happy and sweeping everything underneath the rug. I knelt there waiting for a response, waiting for a word, a sound, but nothing came. I was surrounded by nothing more than silence. I got up and jumped onto my bed. "I'm so stupid" I thought. He's not going to say anything, he doesn't even care. I threw the blanket over my legs and turned on the T.V. It was still early in the morning, so everything on T.V. was paid advertising. I kept scrolling until I stopped on a channel where there was a man preaching. "I'll stop here" I thought. This will put me straight to sleep. I turned towards the wall and brought the blanket all the way up to my chin. I exhaled and closed my eyes. The room was silent, but I could hear the guy preaching. The guy spoke about the wedding of Cana in the Bible. I've heard the story before, and I knew the summary of it. It was when Jesus made water into wine, yeah cool story. The guy kept preaching and said, "most of you just read this story and skip it with no amazement, you just think wow that's a neat story." I giggled on the inside as I thought, this guy gets it. He kept preaching and he said, "but if we really think about what Jesus did, we would be amazed." "The process of making wine is time consuming and filled with long hours of labor." "The seed needs to be planted, the plants need to be watered and pruned, then you need to pick the actual grape and go through this process." "During this process, the grape is completely destroyed of what it used to be, then all those juices sit and wait until its fermented enough to drink." "This five to ten-year process, Jesus accomplishes at the snap of his finger."

The hairs on my back jumped out of my skin, as I heard His voice, God - "Jesse, this is what I desire for you. I want to change your life in an instant. Like the wine, I want to make you new. I want to answer all your questions and show you where I've been when you needed me the most." Will you let me?" Jesse - "God I want to, but I am so broken. I don't even know if this is really you, but if this is you, I give you two weeks. I give you two weeks and then I'm done. I shut my eyes and whispered, "two weeks."

Two weeks

I woke with a roar inside my stomach. Jesse – "Man I'm hungry." I looked around and my room was a mess. I thought back to what happened earlier that day, and it all seemed like a dream, but I knew it was real. I got up and got dressed. I put on my shoes as I thought about if I should go to the cafeteria or not. I knew people would be there and I just didn't want to confront them. I waited until the cafeteria was about to close and sprinted to get food. I knew that no one would be there that late so, I wouldn't run into anyone. I got there with ten minutes to spare. I went through the line and got a sandwich. As I headed over to the tables I saw a group of nicely dressed people and I awkwardly tried to walk passed them to sit by myself. I wonder who they were. I've never seen those kids before. As I sat down, one of the kids at the other table got up and started to walk over to my table. "Oh no", I thought, I probably tried to fight him or something last night. I'll just say sorry and get it over with. Jesse - "Hey, what's up man?" Kid – "Do you want to come sit with us?" Uh, not really, I thought but said, Jesse - "okay sure why not." I got up and sat down with their group. I noticed that they were all nicely dressed so I asked, "did you guys just come back from an event?" Group - "Oh no, we just got back from church and we haven't eaten yet. Jesse - "Oh, church, sounds cool." Group- "What did you do today?" Jesse - "Uh nothing much you know, I slept. Sundays are usually pretty boring." Group - "Well if you're bored you should join our book study." "We're actually going right after dinner." Jesse - "Uh, I don't know. I don't even have the book you guys are reading and I'm sure you are really far along." Group - Actually we're starting a new book today, and we have a box filled with them so no worries, you should come." Now I was stuck. I shouldn't have said my Sunday's were boring now I have to go. Group - "So are you coming?" Jesse - "uh…" My mind raced to find an excuse, but it led me to those two words I whispered before I fell asleep, two weeks. Jesse - "Alright," I told the group, "I'll come." We headed down to the group center. There were about fifteen people there and one leader. Everyone seemed to be really nice. They gave me a book and offered me a soda. We all sat down and began the meeting. People took turns reading the book aloud and discussed each section. The book was titled, *Crazy Love*. It dove deep into the creation story of how distinct, specific, and unique everything and everyone is and how each creation has a purpose whether we see it or not. "Jesse how do you feel about this chapter," asked the group leader. Jesse - "Well I have no idea what my purpose is. Sometimes I feel lost at sea with only a life jacket on, and some days I wish I didn't have that jacket." I can't believe I just said that out loud, I quickly thought. They're totally going to judge me. Group - "Wow dude, that was deep, and I totally have felt that way. I always think of the scripture verse of the disciples being lost at sea and there's a huge storm and everyone is freaking out and Jesus is just sleeping there. Some of the disciples were probably getting mad at Jesus wondering why he was sleeping instead of helping them. Then Jesus wakes up and calms the storm and at the same time he also calms the hearts of the disciples. You see, sometimes we can be in this unknown place lost, scared, and not knowing what to do, but God calls us to become closer to him. Only then we will have peace, and he will bring us calm, even in the midst of chaos. Jesse - "I've never thought about that." The night went on and my curiosity about the book grew. Bible study ended, but before I reached the door, somebody came up to me and said, Team leader - "Hey, you should come again next week? You should also come to our church; I know they are look for people to teach bible study. Jesse - "Uh, I don't know. I'm not very good at teaching the Bible." Team leader - "Dude, I'm not either. It's just middle school kids and I know we could teach them something." Jesse - "Well, uh, okay I'll see you there."

For the next couple of weeks, I received invitation after invitation to many church groups. I was involved with so many groups as I began learning and teaching people about God. A week and a half went by, and my old youth minister from ninth grade called me out of the blue and begged me to come and chaperon a retreat that weekend. I kept trying to find excuses not to go, because I didn't want to be stuck all weekend at a Jesus retreat, but in the end, I couldn't fight it, so I just said "yes." That Friday I drove up to North Georgia to meet the teens. I knew some of these teens from high school and they ran towards me when I got there. Teens - "Dude how's college life?" they asked. "I bet it's crazy huh?" Jesse - "Yeah something like that." We headed down to the conference room to hear the priest give the talk for the night. He spoke about a son who asked his father to give him his inheritance. Once he had it, he ran away and spent it all on girls and gambling, then lost it all. Penniless and broken, the son came back to his father, filthy and repentant. He fell on his father's feet and asked for his forgiveness. He asked to be treated like a servant, for he felt that he no longer deserved to be called his son. The priest ended by saying - Not only did his father not accept him as his servant, but he stood him up and said, "you are my son, and my son you shall be always no matter what." He called his servants to get his son cleaned up and told everyone to get ready for a feast because his son had returned. Tears began to stream down my eyes as I held my head down. All I could think about was my court date, and going to jail, and how I've let everyone down. I have to change. My dad would be so disappointed in me.

The next morning, we got up early to be the first ones in line for breakfast. As we waited for breakfast to begin, I saw my youth minister motioning me with her hand to come over to her table. As I walked over to her, I noticed she was talking to some man. I wondered who he was as I approached their table. Youth Minister- "Hey Jesse this is Tony. He's the mission director here at Life

Teen and hires all the yearlong missionaries for the upcoming year. They have one more spot available." Jesse - "Hey Tony." I shook his hand as my youth minister snuck out. Jesse - "So Tony, what's this mission year about?" Tony - "Well Jesse, I call it dating God for a year, which I know sounds weird but it's a year where your focus is to grow closer to God. Each morning we wake up and pray for about an hour, and then we have formation. We cover a different spirituality books, and section of theology during formation and then the rest of the afternoon we do work base projects and help the local community. It's a whole year, so it's a commitment but hearing from your youth minister about where you are in life, I think this might be good for you. A whole year I thought to myself. I would miss a whole year of school. I wonder what my parents would think. "I just, I don't know," I told him, "I'll have to pray about it." I headed out that very moment to the chapel. I knelt down and laid my forehead on the front pew. "God, I don't know what to do. I still have so many questions and

I am still so angry. I don't know what to do." I sat there in silence and I looked up and said to him, "well I gave you two weeks, and the past two weeks have been amazing." Jesse – "I still have so many questions so here's to a whole year!"

Chapter 5   Letting Go

The year began with a big bang. As soon as I arrived at the camp, the group leader lead us to our rooms and told us to pack our bags for a three-day hike. All the guys in the room looked at each other and shouted, "Heck yeah, this is going to be fun." Tony led the hike. He reminded us that we had about eight miles to cover for the first day so we should take the time to get to know each other as we walk. I was kind of shy and out of breath so I didn't know how much talking I would actually be able to do. The trees were filled with autumn leaves and the wind was brisk to the touch. You could hear the river flowing throughout the curves of the mountains as the birds sang and danced around the trees. Missionary - "Hey, so what's your name?" Jesse - "Uh, hey I'm Jesse, nice to meet you. Are you excited for this year?" Missionary - "Yeah man I'm pumped." "I'm excited to see what it's like." He gave me a weird look as he asked - "So what made you decide to become a missionary?" Jesse – "Well I just… um it's kind of a long story." Missionary – "Well it's kind of a long walk." I didn't know what to say. I didn't want to talk about my life, but there was no way around it. Jesse - "I just feel lost. I've kind of been on my own since I was thirteen and I feel like God has abandoned me and left me out to die. I feel like God has taken everything that is good away from me, and I don't know what I've done to deserve it. I hit rock bottom. I went to jail, but thank goodness that it all worked out, and it was cleared from my record. I guess I'm just looking for answers. I'm looking for purpose, direction, and I don't know, just something like that." Missionary - "Wow man that's crazy." "I'm sure God has a lot planned for you." Jesse - "Yeah, I hope so." The guy then walked away to catch up and speak to someone else. "God has a lot planned for you." These words kept running through my head.

We got to the end of the hike. I could see everyone circling around Tony, so I ran to catch up to everyone. Tony - "Alright guys, we have a pretty big jump here, maybe about twenty-five to thirty feet. We will jump here and continue the hike below to our campground." A jump, sick, I thought. I was pumped. I've never done a jump before off a waterfall like this. Tony- "Before you jump, make sure you look at where you want to jump, aim and then jump." We all got closer to the edge as Tony pointed out areas to avoid. I began to feel a little nervous as I looked to see how far down it was. Rocks deep in the water surrounded the area we needed to jump into, and all I could imagine was me smashing into the rocks. What if I missed where I was aiming to jump? "No way," I said, "I'm not jumping," as I slowly moved to the back of the line. Tony and five others jumped immediately. I could hear them laughing all the way down. One after another they all jumped, until it was my turn. I stepped close to edge. My knees began to shake. Jesse -"Man, this is so high; why do we have to jump?" People began climbing back up to jump over again. It was my turn, and some people began to chant my name below to get me to jump. Jesse – "God, I don't want to jump," I told him, "I'm scared." What if something bad happens?" As the chanting continued, I moved closer to the edge. I looked to where I wanted to jump and then looked up quickly and said, please keep me safe. I pushed off the edge with both of my feet and felt the rush of wind run through my body as I hit the water. I opened my eyes and immediately exhaled with excitement. Jesse - "That was so sick. I want to do it again!"

Night fell quickly, as we finished setting up the camp and began to build a fire. We brought a couple of pots with us and made soup for dinner. The fire began to grow as Tony started his welcome speech. Tony - "Guys, it's going to be a great year. We have a lot planned and more importantly so does God. Everyone is here for many different reasons, but we are all seeking the same thing. I printed out a bunch of quotes from scripture, and I want everyone to pick one from this hat and we will go around in a circle to discuss it. He passed out the hat. I wondered what scripture verse I would get. I reached in and grabbed one piece of paper. I began to read the verse - "I will heal your wounds and bring you back to full health." (Jerimiah 31:17) Mhmm, I thought. Well that's cool. I don't know what wounds I have; the doctors did a pretty good job of fixing them up. The conversation began around the campfire. Slowly but surely everyone shared their quote. I sat their trying to listen to everyone else, but I was confused by my own verse, and I kept thinking about what purpose it served. Tony - "So what's your verse Jesse?" Jesse – "Oh, uh, Jeremiah 31:17. I will heal you from your wounds and bring you back to health." Tony - "Wow, that's a good one. Does anything stand out to you as you read it?" Jesse - "Uh no, not really, I'm actually struggling to understand it." The missionary that I spoke to earlier spoke up and said, "Jesse, I know we were speaking earlier and I don't know man, I just feel like you have so much pain and hurt from your past and so many questions that I think this verse is perfect for you. I think this year God wants to show you and answer all of those questions." "Most importantly God wants to heal you and bring you back to full health, and not physically but mentally, and spiritually!" I didn't know what to say. He spoke with such a depth of truth that I couldn't answer back, so I finally voiced a "yeah, I agree," to make sure they moved on. But he was hundred percent right. I am in pain, and I do have a lot of questions that haven't been answered and I've been running from them my whole life. I miss my Dad. I still lay there at night dreaming of what life would be like if he never died or if I never hurt my leg. Why did God allow me to go through so much suffering? That night I laid in bed and thought about how amazing my day was. I've never had so much fun before and I cannot believe I jumped off that cliff! I can't believe I ever hesitated. I closed my eyes and fell asleep with a smile.

The Depth of Wounds

One of my roommate's name was Dom. He grew up by the beach in Melbourne Florida, and he would always talk about how amazing the food, community, and the beach was. At night, he would tell me these amazing stories as I laid at the top bunk. He would tell me about his family and how amazing his friend group was and that it was simply home. He always said it was the people in that town that made it feel like home. We would stay up late talking into the night, but he seemed to fall asleep before me. His snores would keep me up at times and I would lay there and let my mind wander. I kept thinking about what he said, that it was the people in his town that make it feel like home. My mind took me back to when I was eleven. We were living in an apartment that sat upon a hill. Each day after school I would jump on the bus and catch up with my friends from different grades. One of my favorite parts of riding the bus was right before we got to the apartments, I could see the windows of my room and my sisters' room from a distance. My sister had a bookshelf sitting in front of her window, so her window was always covered, but mine was simply empty. One day when we jumped on the bus, we were just minutes away from our apartment. I looked up to the window and it looked different this time. My sister's window was empty just like mine. The bus came to a stop and the doors opened. I was stuck. I couldn't move. I didn't know what to do. Why was my sister's bookshelf not there? I got up slowly. The bus driver called out my name to remind me that this was my stop. I walked down the steps and the bus drove off. I started to walk towards the apartment, as I see my sister coming out

of our neighbor's house calling my name. Jesse -
"Hey what's going on?" Sister – I don't know. I
guess we can't live there anymore, because we don't
have money. Jesse - "Where's dad?" Sister - "I think
he's trying to figure everything out." We went to
our neighbor's house and waited until our dad
came. I sat by the window, and worried about Dad,
and if he was okay, and where we would sleep that
night. Later that night dad came to the neighbors
and went directly to speak to them. I wonder if we
are going to stay here, or maybe they will let us go
back to our own house. Minutes passed by. Our
neighbor headed up stairs and dad finally came and
met my sister and I on the floor of a room. Jesse -
"Dad, so can we go back home to sleep now?" Dad
- "No son, we're going to have to stay here for a
little bit longer." Jesse - "But why? What's wrong? I
miss home." Dad pulled out a blanket as he looked
at my sister and I and said, Dad - "look at each
other and look at me. This is home. We are each
other's home. No matter where we sleep as long as
we have each other, we are home."

My missionary year started flying by as we started hosting middle school and high school retreats. At times, I felt so intimidated by how much everyone knew about their faith. People would start saying a prayer, so I would move my lips sometimes to pretend like I knew them too, but I had no clue. I wondered how and where they learned so many prayers. During formation, we read different books and made the teaching practical so we could relate to them. One week, we read *The Prodigal Son,* and Tony asked everyone to think about, who you are in the story. Were you the father who accepts and forgives his son? Were you the jealous older brother, or the younger brother that selfishly ran away with all of his inheritance?" After a couple of minutes, one by one, everyone began to share. Everyone said that they were the older brother. Tony - "Jesse what about you?" Jesse - "Uh, well I guess I am the only one, but I feel like the younger brother. I really feel that I relate mostly to the younger brother." Tony - "Well we are all in different places in our lives, but our goal is still the same, to one day be able to be like the father and accept everyone in our lives with open hands and hearts no matter what wrong they have done to us." Those words kept ringing in my head as I thought about my mother out in California, and as I thought about the night my father died, and the words my sister said to me right before. I shook my head and told myself that's all in the past. Stop thinking about it and move on, but as much as I tried those wounds kept surfacing.

I Can Only Run So Far

Summer rolled in, and myself and fourteen other missionaries headed to Boston to lead a couple camps. The first week came by quickly, as the first campers started to arrive. A bus stopped right in front of the camp doors and we cheered for the oncoming campers. As the campers start coming off, I started to notice that it was girl after girl after girl. The leader jumped out and said, "Well, here we are." I looked around. We were surrounded by thirty middle school girls, so I blurted out, "hey, did y'all leave the guys behind? "Haha, no, this is our group for the week," said a girl. Jesse - "Oh, ok." The girls began to laugh as we headed down the stairs to the main stage. The Camp Leader asked the missionaries, "are you all excited to start camp?" Jesse - "Yeah, but is this the only group coming this week?" Camp Leader - "Haha yup, that's it. We were thinking of giving all the guys a break to go out and do other stuff while us girls run most of the session. Jesse - "Sounds good to us." While camp got started, all the guys began planning on what to do while the girls hosted camp. We looked at each other, and of course we started with food. We decided to start our week out by going out to a fancy lunch to eat our hearts out. The next day we headed to lunch. We got to the restaurant and looked around and everyone was wearing button down shirts and dresses, while we were wearing ripped shorts, sandals, and t shirts. Clearly, we did not get the dress code memo. We sat down and the priest who came with us said, "hey guys, I got you covered, just order what you want." We looked at the menu and our eyes grew a bit with excitement. After the waiter took everyone's orders, I began to look around the room. The lighting was low, and the restaurant had intimate booths which made the restaurant seems extremely quiet. The waiter came out with our meals and everyone dove straight into the food. The conversation at the table was great. We began to talk about our future plans, and it made me begin to wonder what I would be doing next. As I was thinking about all of this, a loud noise erupted from our table. You could hear a pen drop as the restaurant grew quiet and everyone looked over to our table. Priest - "Okay guys, who did that? Whoever did that, it is both unacceptable and rude please apologize." Everyone looked over my way, so I said "what, what happened?" Missionary Guy – "Dude, it came from your side just admit it, you farted, man up to it." Jesse - "What? That wasn't me. Dude, it really wasn't me.

We're at a restaurant, I wouldn't do that." Every finger at the table pointed towards me asking me to admit it. My voice grew louder in irritation as I said, "guys, it really wasn't me." The priest then waved his hand over and looked over to the silent restaurant and said, "sorry for the disruption folks, please enjoy your lunch." Chatter erupted all around as I wondered why they were all blaming me. I tried again. Jesse - "Guys, it really wasn't me - look I'm all about a fart but come on, we are at a restaurant I would never do that. Grins grew in every direction as they said, "dude come on, we know it was you." Anger began to stir inside me, and I shouted once more, "dude it's not funny, it really wasn't me." Lunch resumed as if nothing happened. I was fuming inside. I didn't know why everyone was blaming me when I really didn't do it. The rest of the day I replayed what happened at the restaurant in my mind and grew in fury by the minute. What made me even more angry was the thought that someone really did fart and they blamed it on me instead of standing up and admitting that it really wasn't me. Dinner rolled around, and we sat down with the girls. Missionary - "How was the camp session today?" Missionary Girl - "It was great we talked about Jesus and painted our nails." How was lunch? I watched the guys as their faces turned into a grin and with a giggle one of them said, "well it was eventful, and you won't believe what Jesse did…" My face grew hot. I couldn't believe this wasn't over. Jesse - "Guys come on, not in front of the girls," Missionary Girls - "No, tells us what happened," Jesse - "Dude, stop. It really wasn't me. Will you just quit it," I said with a plead in my voice. He ignored me and kept going. Missionary Guy - "Well we were at lunch all enjoying our elegant meal, when someone…" He stopped to look at me. "Erupted with the loudest, most disgusting, fart I've ever heard in my life. It was so loud that it made the whole restaurant stop. Isn't that right Jesse?" They all began to laugh. "That's so gross Jesse," one of the girls said to me. I couldn't hold it back anymore. I erupted with anger, Jesse- "enough, dude it wasn't me. I would never do that, and whoever did do it needs to man up and admit it instead of lying and saying it was me. The laughter continued. Missionary Guy- "Dude it was you, just man up and say it." I could feel it within me. This deep anger engulfed me, and I felt like jumping over the table and punching him across the face. I could feel myself lunging forward, but I stopped. I didn't know why I felt this way. I bit down on my teeth to keep my anger and the tears from coming down. I got up and ran straight downstairs to the chapel. My eyes began to swell as I fell on my knees and screamed inside my head. Why am I so angry?! Why can I not control it? God why am I so angry at something so stupid? I closed my eyes and asked again; God why am I so angry?

I could see myself little again. I was about thirteen, my father had just died, and I was living in a foster home. I could see myself being picked up from the boys and girls club by my case worker. She was driving me back to my foster home. When we pulled up the driveway, I saw the foster mom waiting outside with her hands crossed. We got out of the car and she began yelling at my case worker. Foster Mom – "This boy you brought to my home is a thief. He stole ten dollars from my purse. I had ten dollars in my purse, and now it's gone. He is a worthless thief, and I don't want him in my house." She walked towards me and yelled, "you are a thief, and you will never have a home. Just admit you took my ten dollars." Jesse – "I... I... I didn't take it. I promise. Look inside my book bag." I looked over at my case worker and pleaded with my eyes for her to believe me. I said it again, "I didn't take it." Case Worker - "Well ten dollars just don't walk, away do they?" I looked around me as if my dad would magically appear, but he didn't, he wasn't there. Jesse - "I promise, I didn't take it," I said as tears started rolling down my face. "Foster Mom - "See, he took it, and he feels bad that why he's crying. Take him out of my house." Jesse - "I promise, I promise, I didn't take it."

My hands covered my face with tears as I lifted my head up and look around the chapel and asked, "God, where were you?" I was just a little kid and I didn't do anything wrong. Where were you to stand up for me! My head fell into my lap as tears continued to stream down. "Where were you God?!..." I felt hands wrap around me as I heard his voice in a whisper, "I was right here my son. I know you didn't steal the money. Look at me, I know you didn't take it. I was right here all along, I've always been right here with you." I could feel his embrace and his comfort as I ran to him, as a thirteen-year-old boy. "You believe me," I asked. "Yes, I know you didn't do it." I fell to my knees. I could feel him in every moment when I was suffering. He was there the whole time. I was never alone. When I hurt my arm, He was there in the ambulance. When my dad died, He was right there holding my head as I fell asleep that night. He was right there when I ripped my helmet off in the field. He was right there when I drank my pain away. He was right there when I fell on my knees, begging him to stop taking everything away from me. As He continued to hug me, I felt an overwhelming understanding of my pain and suffering. I understood that pain and suffering was never part of Gods plan. His plan was for all of creation to live in goodness and in harmony but since we have free will, we have the option to cause suffering, and pain. So, what does God do? He allows evil to exist, and by allowing it to exist, he allows us to exist. God doesn't get rid of evil because that would mean getting rid of us when we do something bad, when we sin, and when we fall. As parents we cannot prevent our kids from getting scrape, bumps, or from falling. All we can do in those tear-filled moments is teach our children life lessons. We teach them that things hurt, we teach them that pain sucks, but we teach them to learn from it and to get back up. As the perfect parent, God looks at us in our time of suffering and pain and embraces us with open arms. I'm here, He says, I'm here. As I felt his embrace, I simply understood all of this. I knew I wasn't an orphan, I knew I wasn't abandon, and I knew this life of suffering and pain was never part of Gods plan.

 I've been running away from all my problems and wounds for so long and the answer was always right in front me. I just never took the time to look. I never took the chance to let God in and show me where He was at those times when I needed him the most. He was always there. God's plan was never to make me suffer, but rather, He was there to comfort me during my suffering. My whole life people would tell me this was part of Gods plan, but God never planned for me to suffer but rather during my time of suffering God was there to bring comfort.

Chapter 6 - Down the Mountain

During my mission year every morning at 7 a.m. I would sit in the chapel, praying, and asking God questions. I found myself like a little kid, curious about every little detail. I wanted to know how, and I wanted to know why. Scripture came alive to me. I could understand what was actually going on when I read the bible. I was back from Boston and Summer was ending. Most importantly my year was almost over and I didn't know what I was going to do. That night, a men's retreat was kicking off for the weekend, and I knew that we were expected to go and participate, but I felt so tired, I didn't know how much more I could give. I left the meeting room and headed towards my house. My mind began racing as I felt that I should go back. I have so much to do, I thought to myself. I have to do laundry, and I definitely need a shower, and It would be nice to lay around for once. I tried convincing myself that I should go home, but the more I tried the greater the urge I felt to go back to the retreat. I looked up to the sky and said, "fine you win." I walked back into the retreat room and sat against the back wall, right in time to hear the first speaker of the night. As I sat there, I could feel the coldness of the wall on my back. It felt good, so I laid my head back and closed my eyes as I listened to the first speaker. He asked us to think about how we thought God see's us. Speaker - "I asked myself once, if I died, how would God present me to heaven? If God was presenting me to all of heaven as a game show host would to a crowd, then how would God present me?" As he continued talking, I felt a spark ignite in my mind. "How does God think of me and what would He say about me?" I thought. Speaker - "Okay, now I want everyone to find another guy and share with them your thoughts. Share with them how you think God would present you to all of heaven if you died right now." Well for me it's simple, I thought. He would say here is Jesse he's tired. I laughed to myself. Everyone got out of their seats and started to pair up. I looked around and thought, well everyone will pair up and if there is one person left without someone, I will go be their partner. People began sharing as the speaker said, "I have one more person without a partner, who doesn't have one?" I quickly got up and looked around the room to see if there was anyone else available to partner up with him. No one moved. Hmmm okay, I'll do it. I walked to where he was sitting. He was older, had a lot of gray hair, and he was nicely dressed for a retreat. This guy could be my father. What the heck am I doing here, I thought. I have nothing to offer here. I sat down and introduce myself. Jesse - "So I guess we are sharing how God would introduce us huh?, I said as my voice cracked a little. Man - "Yeah, I guess so." "Uh okay," I said, "I'll go first." "I guess God would introduce me as a kid who has gone through a lot of suffering. A kid who has done a lot of bad things and has run away from everything but maybe overall someone who is trying to be better? I don't know I guess I just feel like God would just be disappointed in who I have been and I'm just trying to make up for all that bad. Man - "Wow, yeah I understand what you are saying. I kind of think the same." Jesse - "So how would God introduce you?" Man – "God would say, here is a man who had a beautiful wife and daughter. But after my daughter died I wasn't the same, I grew angry with God. I hated God so much that I began to gamble, got addicted to other things, and left my wife. His voice started to crack as a tear rolled down his cheeks. I just miss my family. I miss my daughter. God would introduce me as a disgrace and a coward." I put my arm around his shoulder as I sat there praying in my head, "God please lead me, and help me to say what you want me to say in this moment." "It's okay," I said, "it's okay you are here for a reason. Let's pray together. God thank you for bringing us together here today. God I pray for this man and I pray for his sorrows and his pain. God you are a God that heals and a God that loves us so greatly. (The man's cry grew as I continued praying.) Lord, I pray that you heal his heart. I pray for his daughter who is with you." I closed my eyes and I saw a little girl dancing and playing in a beautiful field. I said to the man, "I see your daughter, she is in heaven. I see her dancing around in a field with a smile that brings light. His cry grew louder as other people began to look over to see what was going on. Jesse - "Hey, it's okay. God loves you I know that everything will be okay. Man – "No, no, Jesse you don't understand. My daughter, when I was still married, we had just found out that our daughter had cancer. We were devastated. How could a God give my little daughter cancer? She loved dancing, Jesse. She was so happy when she danced, but her cancer grew so bad that she could no longer walk. One night around 2 a.m., I woke up to her screaming "Daddy, daddy!" I ran to her room and I picked her up and asked, "what's wrong honey?" "Daddy," she said, "daddy I just had the most amazing dream. I was in a beautiful field and I was dancing daddy, I could dance again." The man fell to his knees and said to me, "Jesse, I now know my daughter is in heaven and I need to be a better man so that I can one day be in that field dancing with her." My eyes started welling up with tears, when a priest came over and asked us if everything was okay. "Yes, everything is fine," we said. The man left to speak with the priest as I sat there in tears. God how? Why? I almost didn't come tonight and this man he was so broken. Why would you choose me to help? I sat there in awe. I couldn't believe through all my tiredness and faults God could use me for good. I laid in my bed that night thinking about that man and how broken he was and all I did was pray. I couldn't help but think of how many other people like him were out there. I couldn't help but think of the many nights I've laid in bed hopeless as I cried myself to sleep. I closed my eyes as I thanked God for the night and hoped that one day I could help more people.

A Million Times More

Soon after the men's retreat, Tony came up to me and asked the question, "Jesse what do you feel like God is calling you to next? My mind raced as I looked for an answer, but all I could say was "I don't know yet." Tony - "No worries, it will be clear all in due time." I hope so, I thought. I've never been so lost and confused. I came into this mission year to find myself but in doing so I've lost my vision of what I wanted to do in the future. I prayed for the following weeks asking God to help me and to lead me to where I should go and what I should do next. "God is it another mission year? Is it school? Is it the priesthood?" Later that week as I walked to lunch, I ran into the president of a non profit organization, and out of the blue asked me, "hey Jesse, what are your plans for next year?" Jesse - "hey, uh, I'm not sure yet. I'm still trying to figure that out." President - "Well our non profit is paying for a couple of student scholarships to go to a small university if that's something you are interested in. It does come with a catch though, you have to get involved with the local high school and help with some type of ministry. I think you might like it, and I bet you could coach football there." My eyes lit up as he continued talking. He gave me the number of the person I needed to talk to and I immediately called them. Excitement and joy grew within me, as the coach and school welcome me and expressed their excitement to have me. I headed towards the chapel and prayed, "Thank you."

Fall came quickly, and football season was starting. I met with the head coach of the local football team, and I became the defensive end coach. The next day I met the team as we began to run drills. The team was small. We barely had thirty players and most of them played both sides of the field. I had about three defensive ends and one of them was the quarterback. He was a little cocky as he would always have this grin and this walk that gave off tremendous attitude. "Alright guys, I'm Coach Garcia and our goal this year is to play smart, attack every play, and to never give up." We had two hula-hoops on the floor and I asked them to line up behind the hoop. Jesse - "At the sound of the whistle your goal is to get around this hoop as fast and as close to the hoop as you can." "Ready," (whistle blows). It was funny watching them try to tip toe by the side of the hoop as they tried their best to stay close. It reminded me of when I used to do these very same drills. My high school sophomore year, myself and nine other players made it to the varsity team. It was a proud moment, especially because we were the only sophomore team during the playoffs. The only downside to being on the team as a sophomore, was being the practice dummies for the seniors. One day our coach had us lined up into two lines facing each other. "Okay guys," he yelled, "Oklahoma time." I hurried to look at the opposite line to quickly calculate who I was going to go up against. I always avoided this one person who went by the name of, Cameron Heyward, (who now plays for the Pittsburg Stealers.) He was bigger, faster, and a lot stronger than me, plus my friend's shoulder hurt for a month from going up against him just one time. I gulped, there was no going back. I was going up against him today. "Get angry, you can take him," I thought. I thought about when I was ten years old and a local bully stole my favorite watch and I could feel the anger building inside me because I knew I couldn't do anything about it. I felt the anger rise within me from that memory. He lined up right in front of me, and I grit my teeth. The whistle blew. I exploded off the ground and collided against a train that did not want to be moved. I almost fell backwards as I hit him, but I held my ground. The whistle blew to stop the play. I shook my head, and walked back to the line. "That wasn't that bad, my head is spinning, but that wasn't that bad," I said to myself. After that moment, I believed in myself. I knew if I could take a hit from Cameron Heyward I could take on anyone. I blew the whistle and said, "okay guys, this time lean into it, drop your shoulder and run as fast as you can around it." I blew the whistle and watched them run the drill, as I thought to myself, "how do I get them to not just believe in me as a coach, but to believe in themselves."

The season kicked off with a great start. We were plowing through teams. Each day I looked for the opportunity to perfect my coaching in little ways. Every chance I got, I learned more and more about how to develop the human person on and off the field. These kids weren't just football players, they were sons and they were students. They had more than what football had to offer and I knew it was a great lesson for them to translate into their own life. School helped me to be the coach and the man I wanted to be, as I dove into philosophy and theology. I became more and more obsessed with reading and questioning everything. I didn't question for the sake of questioning, but rather I wanted to find truth, I wanted to have a solid foundation for my life. Every week I translated what I learned into how I coached my players. Every week I was astonished by how much everyone grew. Week after week, I could see the transformation of my players on and off the field, as I watched them come alive during each game we played.

We all sat around the locker room. The players began to put their helmets on. Offensive Coach- "Okay, captains to the field. Now guys this is the game we've all been waiting for, The State Championship. All summer long, we've been waiting for these forty minutes. Forty minutes to achieve what this school has never achieved. You have forty minutes and for you seniors these might be the last forty minutes you ever play in football. Forty minutes to bring to life, all the sprints, all the weight lifting, and all the long practices to showcase your best talents. Now's the time to show our whole school that we are a championship team. Let's go out there and win this thing!!!" We kicked off first quarter. I sat in the booth with my headset on. Our Quarterback scrambled for a touchdown and we scored first. I began to anticipate the other team's strategy. They would run the ball a couple of times and go for a play action and catch our linebackers sneaking up. Our defensive of ends were rushing so far up field, that they would push themselves away from being able to make a play. The opposing team scored as half time rolled in. We headed towards the locker room everyone broke off into their special team. I grabbed the defensive ends and told them, "look guys this team knows you guys are really fast. They are just letting you run down the field and then they are running right between the tackle. What I need you guys to start doing is as you come off the ball put your inside hand on the outside of the tackle and quickly read the play. The running back will either try to run outside of you or inside. As soon as you see him make the cut, hit that gap. Now if it's a pass, just act like the hula-hoop is on the ground and get around that tackle as fast as you can. Remember, don't run straight run the hoop. Now look at me. If we do this, we win the game. We are better than this team. Let's go out there and win this game!"

The second half kicked off, and the opposing team received the ball. I stood up and looked at the game from the booth. "Come one guys, play smart," I thought. They snapped the ball. They gave the running back the ball. He tried to cut inside, because he expected the defensive end to be down the field on the outside, but he hesitated. The Defensive End cuts inside and tackles the running back for a loss. Jesse - "That a boy, now that's how we play football." Our Defensive End stopped them as we returned the punt for about ten yards. In just fifteen minutes into the game, both defense looked unstoppable. We couldn't run the ball, and each time we tried to pass it out, the Quarterback was rushed to throw it away. It was the fourth quarter and there were only about five minutes left on the clock. We ran a quick pass play out to the flat, and I noticed that our Tight End was wide open. A couple plays later, we ran the same play and same thing happened, he was wide open. I looked over to the offensive coach and said – "tell our Quarterback to run that same play again, but this time to look for the Tight End." He had been open every single play. The clock was down to two minutes. The ball was snapped. The Quarterback took a five step drop as our Tight End clears the Linebacker and our Quarterback throws the ball. Our Tight End catches it at the five-yard line and gets tackled before he could score. The crowd roars as the offense runs a quick play up the middle to score. Touchdown, touchdown!!! I look at the clock and see there are only forty seconds left. "Okay, we can do this. We just need to hold them off for forty seconds." We kick off the ball, and they return it to about the twenty-five-yard line. We line up in a safe defense with three Safeties deep and three Defensive Ends. They hiked the ball, and the Quarterback scrambles and gets tackled inbound. They have no time outs so they rush back to the line to snap a play. The clock ticks down to ten seconds. "Hike!" The ball is snapped and the Quarterback drops back. Seven seconds. Our Defensive End runs around the tackle, as the Quarterback scrambles to avoid getting tackled. Four, three, two, their Quarterback throws it right up in the air, as our safeties jump at the right moment and knock it down! That's it! We won! We won the state championship!!! We run down from the press box to join the team. We won! We ran onto the field jumped in the air. We're state champions!

That night I laid in bed as the whole game, season, years, replayed in my mind. I couldn't help but to think of him also. I missed him. I wondered what he would have said to me after the game. Jesse - "I hope I'm making you proud dad."

Chapter 7 Trouble with Love

Football season was over so I started to look for an internship. I began calling churches and sending emails, until one church picked up and oddly enough they were looking for an intern. The church was just down the street from where I lived and I couldn't feel more loved by God. I called my girlfriend at the time and I let her know that I got the position and she was super excited for me. She was actually moving to a school closer and we would now be able to see each other more often. I remember the first time I ever met her. One of my friends from high school invited me to come to church with her one night. We got there early and she knelt down to pray as I stared off into space. The room grew with a voice singing traditional hymns. The sound of her voice moved my eyes towards her and I locked eyes with her. My heart stopped. The vibrations of her voice awoke my soul. "Uh Pamela, Pamela, who is that?" I nudged her as she looked up. "Oh that's my friend, she looked at my face and continued, "I'll introduce you after mass." Jesse - "Okay cool." I sat deep into my seat as I felt like Mandy Moore in the movie *A Walk to Remember* was singing to me. Mass finished after an hour and the pews slowly emptied as we waited for my introduction. Pamela got up and I slowly followed behind like a kid hiding behind his mom as she tries to show him off. "Hey Katie this Jesse, Jesse this is Katie," she said. I shook her hand as I stuttered, "uh that was good song, I mean singing."

Katie - "Thanks." Not much happened after that, but I didn't blame her, I totally made a fool out of myself, but I remember that day like it was yesterday.

I drove to the Church to see where I would be working. As I walked into the teen room, there were around two hundred pictures glued to the right side of the wall. The pictures were of all different faces. Youth minister -"Hi, you must be Jesse." Jesse - "Hi, yeah, I'm so excited to be here." I looked over as Andrew walked over to me and just gave me the greatest hug. "What's up man? How's life after the missionary year?" Jesse - "It's good man, it's just different, definitely hard to get used to." Andrew- "Oh I know man, when I did mine four years ago I had the same feeling, glad you're here though." We all sat down and they told me more about the Church. Youth Minister - "So why did you call? Did someone tell you that we had a position open? Jesse – "Not at all, I was looking for work." Youth minister - I guess it's just God then. "So Andrew will be stepping into my position, because I will be leaving to enter into the consecrated life to hopefully become a nun, and we just started talking about who would take his position. Jesse - "Hahaha, that's awesome." I couldn't help but laugh, they awkwardly laughed with me. Jesse - "Well I'm excited! What's the pictures on the wall??" Youth Minister- "That's all our teens. We take a picture of them so we can try and remember their names." Jesse - "Oh wow that's a lot of teens." Youth Minister - "Ya, we have a lot." Jesse - "That's awesome!" Youth Minister- "Yeah, we have so many teens during our Sunday event that we have a core team of adults that helps us. Our weekly schedule looks like this - Wednesday we have bible study - Thursday we have theology discussion, and Sunday is our big night where everyone comes." I could already tell that she was a very detailed orientated person and she stayed on top of things. That following Sunday I was going to be introduced as the new intern to the whole youth group. As I drove to the church I could feel my nerves tighten and my stomach began to feel funny. When I got to the gym floor, the room was filled with the sounds of a couple hundred teenagers. I looked around to find a familiar face. I then noticed the youth minister talking with other adults in a corner. "Oh, that must be the core team," I thought. I walked over to the group and she greeted me, "Hey Jesse. Team this is our new intern Jesse." I shook everyone's hand one by one. They greeted me kindly, and some even came in for a hug. Youth minister - "Jesse, this is our core team. You might have noticed that for some this is a part time job, and some are in college that have graduated from here actually just a couple years ago. One girl immediately came over to me and gave me a great big hug. I guess she knew my girlfriend but at the time, I had no idea who she was. "Hi," she said, "I'm Elizabeth." Jesse - "Uh, hi." Elizabeth- "Ya, I'm friends of your girlfriend. I met her during our summer missionary year." "Shoot, that's why she looked so familiar. She was one of the summer missionaries," I thought. Jesse - "Oh ya, I remember you. How's have you been?" Elizabeth - "Yeah, everything is going great! Just going to school and church. Ya it's good. How about you?" Jesse - "Well kind of the same, going to school. I just finished coaching, which was great. We won the state championship but now I'm here. Elizabeth - "That's awesome. Yeah, I'm excited for tonight." I walked away to grab water and couldn't help but think about how small of a world it is and how everyone I knew seemed to connected with each other. The night went on without a hitch. I got along with the teens well. They laughed at my jokes, and that's when I knew these were great kids.

Months passed by, and we began to get ready for our big fall retreat. Everyone at the church kept telling me how these particular retreats were special and life changing. I was pumped to be part of it. I've been to a lot of retreats and ran my fair share of them so I couldn't think what made this church retreat better. We had weekly meetings leading up to the retreat and made sure everyone knew what their role was. The biggest night of the retreat was Saturday, because it was filled with praise and worship, the best speakers, and adoration. We had one hundred and fifty teens to plan for and I could tell some people were getting a title bit stressed. The planning became more and more detailed and personalities began to clash. I stood back and watched them argue about who would drive and who wouldn't. I watched and laughed on the inside as things became unnecessarily complicated and quickly decided to interject. "There is no point arguing over who's going to drive or not," I said. "Some people might need to get back early so we can have the bus and I'll have my car if anyone who needs to come back earlier is welcome to ride with me." The teens arrived the next day, and we started the drive up the mountain. It was great to be back at the camp that I'd spent my missionary year. It felt like home. The teens settled into their rooms as the night kicked off. Really, the whole weekend was amazing. The Core Team was right; this was one of the best retreats I had ever been on. Retreats always wore me out. There were long nights and early mornings, and on top of that you had to make sure to set two hours aside for an intense ultimate Frisbee match. Sunday rolled around and just like that it was time to head home. That morning, Elizabeth came up to me and asked if she could drive down with me, because she needed to get back earlier. Jesse - "Ya of course, let's leave in a couple of hours." My favorite session of the retreat by far was the Sunday morning talk, partly because I got to lead it, but mostly because of how important it was. I've seen a lot of retreats and have seen many people go through some great experiences but none of it matter if you do not choose to do something about it. When you get back home you are not supposed to be the same, because you have grown. We have to allow ourselves, when we go back home, to continue to grow. We have to put ourselves in a situation where it nurtures growth and helps us to become the best person we possibly can be. I remember right after my missionary year, I went home and stayed there for about two weeks until school started. I went over to a friend's house and they were doing drugs, taking shots, and just acting dumb. I looked around as everyone was talking and laughing and it felt so quiet. People were talking but they weren't saying anything, people were laughing but I could see the pain behind their laughter. I remember how weird it felt to be at a party like this. It's not that I didn't like the people or that I didn't like to have fun, but I've been here before and I know where it led me and I didn't want to be that person any more. Growth. Growth is one of the hardest things that happen in life because it is such an internal thing that people can easily overlook it. So we continue to live into who people remember us for, and because of this, it is so hard to change. I ended my talk by saying, "If you do one thing when you get home make sure you tell people you are different, you are not the same, you are new, and tell people by your actions and then use your words when needed." I grabbed my bags and texted Elizabeth to meet me by my car. We drove down the mountains with the radio blaring music.

"What a retreat huh?" - Elizabeth "ya you have no idea" "these retreats have save my life" "they are so good I wish everyone could go to them." Jesse - ya man I agree, that was super sick, I just hope those kids pursue greatness and continue to grow. Elizabeth - "gosh me too." Jesse - "so how's school going are you enjoying everything." Elizabeth - "ya it's great I just hate living at home." "I'm in college but I don't really get that college life experience you know?" Jesse - "ya, oh man I don't know if I could do that, but hey at least you safe money since you don't have to pay for a dorm room." Elizabeth- "yup yup that's definitely a plus." Jesse - "so how do your parents feel about it are they pretty cool." Elizabeth - "uhhhh I don't know." She grew quite as she looked outside the window as if she was looking for an answer. Jesse - "what do you guys just not get a long." Elizabeth - no it's not that it's just that my parents have always had a bad relationship and I have no idea why they aren't divorce at times. I just, I don't know my father is so angry at times that he hits my mom and sometimes me and.. " - her voice began to crack as I reach over to turn the volume down. Jesse - oh Elizabeth no, he hits you? Tears streamed down her eyes as she nodded her head. My heart grew with anger as I looked for words to say. We'll look we have do something about this because that's not acceptable does it still happen? Elizabeth - no, no, not anymore but it just effects the way I see God and my relationship with guys. I guess it just takes me longer to trust. My heart grew with anger that someone, her own father would treat her that way. I opened up and shared my story with her. I walked her through my joys, my tears and sorrows. I told her my healing moments and how close I am to God and that no matter what happens he is always there for us. She nodded her head a lot and said "hmmm" a lot. I must of talked a lot because in a blink of a moment we were back to the church. Jesse - Look Elizabeth if anything if you need anything just call me here is my cell phone call if you ever need help. I drove back home that night so happy that I could help her. I sat in my car before I went up and just prayed. God please keep her protected, keep her from harm and let her feel your presence, amen.

Blindsided

It was a Wednesday. I looked forward to Wednesday's because the teens would gather to talk and ask really hard questions about our faith. Some questions were even too big for me to answer, so I would help them come to the self-revealing answer through more questions and more conversation. If God wants us to know Him more, than coming to the truth about Him must be self-revealing. I just had to look. Bible Study was packed. The teens were eating pizza and drinking soda as I handed out the Bibles. We would always read the scripture verses that would be read on Sunday and dove deep into each one. One of our teens raised his hand and asked, "If God knows everything and knows we are going to sin and will turn away from Him, then why does He create us and how could He possibly still love us?" My heart beat grew faster and my palms

began to sweat as I thought about the questions.
Jesse - "Uh wow, yeah, that's a great question. Does
God know everything that will happen? Of course,
He does, He is God, and He doesn't force us to love
Him but we simply have the choice to. So, at every
moment of our life, we have to make choices. We
make hundreds of choices a day, and some of those
choices pertain a good outcome or a bad outcome.
Therefore, we can always at any moment choose
good or bad, but what's awesome is that no matter
what we choose God is still with us. He will always
lead us towards the good. Even if God knows we
will never turn to Him, He will never give up on us.
You will never be able to say, "God gave up on
me," because he will always be there no matter
what." I sat back on the couch and exhaled deeply.
Just as we turned to the next scripture verse, the
door room opened. Everyone turned to see who it
was. In walked Elizabeth. I was surprised to see her
and started to tell her to get a Bible and join us, but
before I could finish in walked in my girlfriend and
another of her friends. I got up to greet them, Jesse -

"hey I didn't know you were..." Girlfriend - "Hey Jesse, we need to talk outside right now. " Jesse - "Wait, what's wrong?" Girlfriend - "Nothing, we just all need to talk outside right now okay?" Jesse - "Uh ya sure. I'm just in the middle of leading Bible Study now. You'll have to wait until I'm done." The teens looked confused at what was happening. I turned my attention back to Elizabeth and my girlfriend, Jesse -"look I don't know what's going on but it's going to have to wait until Bible Study is over." They left and I turned back to the teens, "Sorry guys, they just have a quick question to ask me. Let's keep going with that last verse..." The Bible Study picked up again, and I let some of the core members lead and gathered my thoughts about what had just occurred. I couldn't think of why they seemed so upset with me. Did I do anything wrong? I thought about it and couldn't think of anything I had done wrong. Why was Elizabeth with my girlfriend? My mind kept running in circles at what those girls wanted. I looked at the clock to see how much time we had left for Bible Study. Two minutes. Okay, I can get through this. "Okay, guys we have to wrap up now. For next week make sure you bring in a dollar present for our white elephant Christmas party. Remember don't spend more than a dollar and it can be silly or nice. Let's pray." Prayer ended and the teens headed home. I waved goodbye as their parents drove them home. Time to figure out why the girls were here. I headed down the hallway to meet them outside. Jesse - "Uh, hey, so what's going on." Girls - "Well sit down. We need to talk to you." Jesse - "Uh okay, but what is this all about." Girlfriend- "Well I was talking to Elizabeth and she was telling me how you shared your whole story with her in the car when you guys were coming back from retreat. She said that you poured your whole heart out to her and that's not cool. That's like cheating." My head shook, as I was at lost for words. Elizabeth- "Yeah Jesse, you shared a lot of stuff that you should only be sharing with your girlfriends or your wife." "What?!" I said, Jesse - "Elizabeth you told me your dad was being abusive to you, what was I supposed to say. Oh that's ok go talk to a girl about it?" I was so confused. "All I wanted to do was to share my story not for the sake of sharing it, but with the hope that it could show you how God works even in the darkest of times Elizabeth," Elizabeth - "Ya, but Jesse, you can't do that. You can't share stuff like that with other girls because then you are connected with them. Girlfriend - "Yeah that's like cheating emotionally. You can't do that." As they were talking and ganging up on me, I felt stunned. I felt like I couldn't think or move. I had been completely blind sighted, and it wasn't fair. Girlfriend - "You can't do things like that Jesse. It's like cheating. Just admit you're a cheater." I got up, because I couldn't hold back the tears that were about to come down. I grit my teeth and manage to get a few words out. Jesse - "I, I have to go." Girlfriend - "Ya, that's right. Just run away like you always do!" I got into my car and tried to regain my composure. How, or what did I do God? I was only trying to help. That night I couldn't help but cry. I couldn't help but feel awful. I couldn't help but feel lost. I opened my

phone to the notes sections and wrote this poem.

Regret
Mindless games start with wounded hate
These wounds of your pass arise at last
As the allegory of the cave hides his name
We walk blindly filling up this world with such pain
As we lay in our bed the silences rushes through our
veins
Entering way beyond our brain
Unleashing and unlocking the imprint of His Holy
name
Screaming out I died for you so sin would be your
fame
You see me on this cross and you look at me lame
But you have to idea that I did this for your sake
As I watch you fall it is my tears that makes it rain
Because before you were even born I loved you
I'm sorry for the wrong ways this world has brought
you
But please understand I don't wanna fight you
For I die every second when you think I don't love
you

I look at my hands and see two worlds
one with the power to beat and hurt
And the other with the power to heal and restore
Because it is my hands that opens this destructive
door
It is I that allows you to get beaten to the floor
Because I rather satisfy my desires than love you

even you more
I ruined your purity, your innocence that you had
since birth
I stepped on your identity and made you forget your
worth
I just picked you up and put you down as I do my
telephone
And I regret every second down to my bones
I pray to God that he restores your beautiful soul

My Mind blown as truth unleashes its wrath
I can't believe looking at past and knowing its fact
And sometimes I think should take this step and let
this world be something I left
Endless falling has brought me to my knees
To finally hear what my whole being has been
asking to me to stop and feel
To step behind myself and see what my words and,
interaction are saying in real
To look beyond my intention and too see how they
are received
It doesn't matter if I mean the best If they are
received the wrong way
I was the biggest advocate to fight for women's pure
state
But I myself when I talked with them wasn't being
emotionally chase
Entering into a place where our souls were
connected like a couple on their honeymoon date
Because there are ideas and memories that your
spouse should be the only one allowed to enter that
gate

And thats why I scream and cry because for me it's too late
I do I do I wish now that I would have waited
But now all this love we had is now faded
So here I am standing in front of you so listen I'm about to say it
I love you but I know we'll never make it
Because you deserve better I'm not gonna sit here and fake it
Because all I've done is giving you a heart full of hatred
I rather see you smiling then to simply talk to you for a second
But please understand the way I was raised
At an early age, I would wake up to see my mom with her sex mate
When she was gone my babysitter would change My whole fate
By pulling me close man I didn't even understand the word rape
That's why I don't even know how to treat a woman yes, it's hard say
But it's time that I stand up and stop running away
Women it is you that holds the key
To show us men how to simply be
To be able to love you selflessly and wash your feet
Because with your words and actions you make us weak
You are bone of bones flesh our flesh men and women are meant to be
You are the most beautiful creation that's why Satan went after Eve
So women this is for you please don't think I'm

trying to be mean
But I ask you on this second please teach us how to
uphold your dignity
Show us how to not love you so recklessly teach us
how to look at you with such purity
So that every second you don't have insecurity.
Because when I look at you I want you to see your
true identity

But most of all we need to understand that we are
not defined by our past
So scream at the top of your lungs free at las free at
last
For today I choose to rise up
better yet I choose to men up
To leave all these childish things behind
To quit looking back and walk in this straight line
To fight against these lies and challenged your
minds
To set this world on fire, more than before,
Because yes we are young
So join me and scream at the top of your lungs
Because one day your lungs will breath its last
breath
And on that day, there will be one last word at the
tip of your tongue that will be left
and that word is
Regret!

Chapter 8 - Creating good out of a bad situation

I didn't see much of Elizabeth and I was no longer
with my girlfriend, so I stayed focus on school and
youth ministry. My classes began to intensify as I
took harder courses. We began learning about
freedom and my professor proposed a question. "I
want you to define freedom." Everyone began to
share their answers, but I stayed quite wanting to
listen to everyone else. Most answered that freedom
was having the ability to do as we desired. Others
argued that freedom was choosing to do good. Our
professor looked at us and said, "well let's add
some context. Let's say there was a young boy and
he went up to the piano and he began to bang
around the piano making painful noises. Some
might see this as beautiful. Now imagine the same
situation but this time a young girl goes up to the
piano and begins to play Mozart and Beethoven.
Now in these stories who is freer? The boy banging
on the piano keys, or the girl playing a classical
piece? My mind began to race as I immediately

wanted to shout the boy, but I kept thinking could it be the girl? Student - "Well of course it's the boy, he is not restricted by Mozart and Beethoven. He has the freedom to bang on the piano keys if he wants to. The professor answered, "well the girl can bang around the keyboard too but..." Jesse - , "...but she doesn't choose to right?" Professor- "Correct, Mr. Garcia. Think of it this way. If we replaced the young boy with a monkey or even a dog, could that animal return the same results?" Everyone - "Well, ya of course." Now what about the girl? If we replaced her by a monkey or dog could they return the same results?" The class was silent. "Now this class," continued the Professor, "this is freedom of excellence. Knowledge does not restrict us, but allows us to be freer. Lack of knowledge is the lack of being free. The whole day I walked aimlessly around, as I kept thinking of the Professors analogy. I kept asking myself, am I really free?

Summer came quickly and the end of my sophomore year. I was taking summer classes as it was time to register for next year. One morning, I heard a loud bang on the door that woke me up. I ran to the door and opened it. It was an administrator from my college. Jesse - "Uh, hi." Admin - "What are you still doing here?" Jesse - "What do you mean? I'm taking summer classes?" Admin - "Sure, but you were supposed to be out of the schools housing by now. You need to pack your stuff up and leave now." Jesse - "But why? I paid for the whole summer. You can't do that." Admin - "Look, all I know is that you're going to need to get all of your stuff out and leave by today." Jesse - "Wait, wait I am so confused, why? What's going on?" Admin - "I can see you're not understanding what I am saying. Why don't we go to the school and figure it all out." I grabbed my keys from the counter and jump into my car. As I drove to the school, I thought about where I would live. "I could go back to my parents, but they lived so far away from my job. It was an hour each way. Why are these people even doing this to me? The school had a partnership with the apartment complex. They were our "dorms," so maybe the partnership ended? I don't know, but what I do know is that I was going to have to find a new place to live. I got to the school, and they told me that there was nothing they could do, even though I paid for the whole summer. I needed to move out. I headed back to the apartment, and began packing my car with all of my things. I posted a quick note on the Facebook page of the church group that I was an intern for, and asked if anyone had any advice or if they could help in anyway with my situation. I had just finished packing, when this couple reached out to me and said that they had a spare bedroom that I could stay in until I could get on my feet again. Their house was only minutes away from the church, and I could keep working. It was the best news that I had heard in a while. The way the school treated me left me with a bad taste in my mouth, so I began to look at other school to attend. When I got to work, everyone started to ask if I was okay, and if I found a place to live. I told them I was okay, and found a temporary living situation. The youth minister sat me down and talked to me about what had happened. Jesse - "Yeah, I just can't believe a Christian school would treat someone like that. That's really the most upsetting part about it to me. We are trying to make a difference in the world and then you have people who call themselves Christian but really don't act like it." Youth minister- "That is one of the biggest problems Jesse. People call themselves Christian and then leave a bad impression on people who have no idea what it means to have faith, to have hope, and to have love. For me, I would rather say that I am trying to be Christian then to say I am, because then it makes a distinction. Jesse - "I know what you mean, and I'm trying not to feel hurt about it, but I am. I guess, I just expected more. I just don't know what to do now about school." Youth minister - "Well you should definitely check out the university I graduated from. It's down in Florida. It's a great school! The professors are the best, and the people are great also. You should definitely apply. I went home later that day and applied. Summer was almost over, and I needed to make a decision pretty quickly, but I also needed to talk to my parents about it. I knew they would be hesitant with me deciding to go down to school in Florida. A week went by, and I was accepted to the school and my financial aid went through. I sat on the couch, and looked at my computer screen, "accepted" it read. I felt excited but hesitant. I would have to leave everything behind, my job, my ex-girlfriend, who I still had feelings for, and all my friends. I don't know anyone in Florida. I called my parents, and we talked for hours about what I should do. Parents - "At the end of the day Jesse, we just want you to have a great education and to be happy." Jesse - "I know, and I really think this will be the school for me." Mom - "Well than that's that isn't it? But this is it, no more transferring Jesse." Jesse - "Haha, okay. I promise." So that was it then. I was headed down to the sunshine state of Florida. I googled my school, to see what was around it. It was thirty minutes from the beach, a mall, and a couple of churches. I couldn't believe I would be near the beach again! The ocean always reminded me of when I was little. Once a month, we would go to the Santa Monica Pier and run around. All my siblings and cousins would come, and it would be fun. I loved the ocean and the waves that always came crashing in. My dad and I would always sit right by the water, and he would tell me stories of when he would fish and swim in El Salvador. I could see the joy in his eyes as he gazed into the water. Jesse - "Dad, why do you like the ocean so much." Dad - "Oh Jesse, that is a hard question," he responded. Silence consumed him as I could see him trying to come up with the perfect words to explain how he felt about it. After a while he said, "Jesse, the ocean is filled with wonder and mystery, but for me, it always reminds me of God's infinite love for us." I giggled, and said, "God's love? How?" Dad - "Each time we look upon the ocean, it is never the same. Some days the waves are big and they roar onto the shore, some days it's so still and flat that you could almost see the curve of the earth, and some days the tide is so far out that you can barely see any waves.

But no matter the tide, the waves always find their way back to shore. They are always flowing and moving, and that my son reminds me of God love. In the days that I think He is nowhere near, the ocean, helps me to remember that He is and always will be at the shore waiting for me.

Young, Wild, and Free

I could hear the pavers hitting the tires as I lifted my head off the backseat window. A row of palm trees greeted my eye. Jesse - "Are we here?" Mom - "Yup! Welcome to your new school Jesse!" My heart dropped to my stomach as I thought about all the new people I would have to meet. I wondered if I would get along with my roommate. I wondered if classes would be hard. I hoped they would have a youth group. The car stopped and my mom and I got out. Jesse - "Whoa it's hot out here." It felt like I opened up the oven with my face to close to it and got blasted with hot air. I grabbed my bags and checked in. My new dorm room was actually a suite on the second floor, which meant I would have five other roommates. Hmm, I thought, this should be interesting. As I headed towards the dorm, I heard my name being yelled. "Jesse!" I looked around, and saw a short, blonde girl walking up to me. Jessica - "Hey are you Jesse?" Jesse - "Uh hey. Ya, I'm Jesse." Jessica- "Hi, I'm Jessica. I used to go to high school at the school you coached football in Atlanta." Jesse - "Oh wow, cool. Sorry I must have a bad memory; I don't remember meeting you last year." She giggled and said, "no, no, I graduated the year before you coached, but one of my friends knew you and told me you were coming to Ave too and to reach out to you." Jesse- "Oh, you're that Jessica." Yeah he told me to reach out to you too. So sorry I haven't yet, it's been a crazy day." Jessica- "Yeah same here. It's weird being at a different college this year, and it's so hot here huh? Jesse - "Yeah, its like stupid hot." I looked into her eyes and they felt like I was on a diving board jumping into the clear blue sea. Jesse - "Uh, how's your mom?" I can't believe I just said that, I thought. She laughed awkwardly and said, "uh she's good." Jesse - "Good good. Well sorry, I better find my dorm so I can move all my stuff in and yeah. It was really nice meeting you. I'll see you around." I waved good bye as she walked towards the cafeteria. Gosh I felt so stupid I can't believe I asked how her mom was and I don't even know her mom. I got to my dorm and pushed the door open. Three guys were sitting on the couch playing "Call of Duty" and I immediately knew this was going to be a great dorm. I waked in and dropped my bags and introduced myself to everyone. Jesse - "So is there any beds left." Roommate 1- "Yeah man, you have the last bed it's the back right. Jesse - "Awesome thanks. I'm going to put my stuff up." My room was nice. It had a big window, two beds and two dressers. One of the beds laid parallel against the far back wall and my bed laid horizontally to the wall to the left. I jumped onto my bed and looked out the window. You could see most of the campus. There were three main academic buildings that were to the left, and the church stood tall and bold in the center of the town. It looked like the toy box Buzz Lightyear came in. I mean it really did look like a space ship. I couldn't wait to go inside! I finished unpacking the car and drove my mom to the airport. Before she left she told me "Study hard and be yourself and everything else will take care of itself." I hugged her goodbye and drove off. The car ride went quickly as I drove back to school. I can't believe this is my third college in four years. Man, what a ride it has been. I can't imagine where I would be if my adoptive parents hadn't taken me in. I got back to school and headed back to my room. My roommate was asleep already, and I could hear him snoring softly. I hope his snoring doesn't get any louder, I thought.

The next day I woke up to the warm touch of the sun. I laid there in bed and thought about what I should do. Maybe I should hang out with all my roommates today? Hmm, or maybe I can go to the… Ohhhhh I got it! I have to go get involved with the local youth group! I scrambled out of bed and began asking everyone at the school about how to get involved. I should go to the cafeteria, I thought, that's where I'll be able to find people to ask. I waked over to the cafeteria, and I saw a pamphlet on the wall advertising events for the week. Cool a concert on Friday. Looks like everyone will be going to the bars that night. Then in big bold letters, *Youth Group: Join Us Tonight.* That night I found myself in a fifteen-passenger van with three other people and I couldn't help but say to them, "hey guys, think we should have taken the school bus, there isn't enough room in here." "Hahah!" One of the other guys laughed, but the rest of the van stayed quiet. The road to the local town was filled with farm lands. You could see nothing but rows and rows of crops for miles. Jesse - "Hey guys, would you mind telling me more about this youth group and town?" Youth group student leader - "Yeah man, of course! So this town is one of the poorest towns in all of Florida. It is made up of mostly farm workers and these kids live in rough conditions. Most of the kids don't really like going to youth group, but they go to get food. The church is mostly Hispanic, and the youth minister is a mom who has volunteered to do the job. We've been coming and helping out for about a year. Our goal is to make sure the kids are getting the education and formation that they need and that they can relax, and enjoy their time here." He continued to talk to me, but my eyes wandered and as I looked outside. I was suddenly reminded of where I grew up. You could see people carrying their groceries as they walked home with their children. Older men, with works boots and shirts covered in sweat and dirt. Kids playing outside and running around. Watching these people as our van rode by made me think about playing with all my cousins when I was little. In our apartment complex, there was a large wall that served no specific function. It was about six feet high and about nine feet wide. We would grab a big blanket from our apartment, and some brooms and build a fort. We would play tag and if you were touching the fort you were safe. One time we all ran towards the fort and we ran into it so hard that it all came crashing down on us. We fell beside each other and we could not stop laughing. We laughed so hard one of my cousins started crying..."

Youth Student Leader- "Jesse... Jesse..." Jesse - "Hey, ya, oh we're here." I got out of the car and looked around. The church parking lot was packed. Jesse - "So is this just youth group or are there other events going on in the church." Youth leader - "Yes, there are other events going on." We went into the youth room and it was filled with teens eating, talking and taking selfies. We introduced ourselves to the youth minister and she told us to mingle with the kids, and get to know them and that would be the biggest help for her. I grabbed a piece of pizza and sat down with a group of kids. Jesse - "Hey, I'm Jesse. I go to the local college. Where do you y'all go to school? Teens - "Southside High." Jesse - "Cool, cool. Are you guys any good at football?" Kid 1 - "Yeah, we're pretty good. We went to the playoffs last year, but got beat." Kid 2- "Yeah, but one of our players is going to FSU to play football. He's going to make bank when he goes pro." I laughed a little and said, "well that's cool. How's school? Do you have good teacher?" Kid 3- "Yeah, school's okay, but it's so boring and pointless, and I don't get why we have to go." Youth Minister- "Alright everybody, throw away your trash and come to the front, we are going to begin the night. Please welcome all of our college student helpers and make sure to get to know them and ask them what it's like to be college." The topic of the night was suffering and the challenges we face that can make us sometimes feel mad at God. I nodded my head and laughed inside. We broke up into small groups after she was done speaking and I had my own group of about seven teens. Jesse - "So, what did you all think of the talk?" Kid 1- "It was good, it's just hard." Jessse - "Hard in what sense?" Kid- "It's just like… for example, my grandpa died a year ago and like you don't want people to die and it makes you angry at God, but you have to remember it's a part of life and that they are in a better place." Jesse – "Yeah, I agree with you, anyone else? Kid 2- "I think it's hard that God just puts so much on us even though we are just kids." Jesse - "And what do you mean by that?" Kid 2- "There's like seven people living in our little one bedroom apartment, and I am the only one that can work." Her voice became raspier as she said, "I am the only one that works in my family. I go to school and then I go straight to Wendy's and I don't get out of work until 11pm and then I go to sleep and wake up and do all over again." Tears began streaming down her cheeks. "I'm sixteen years old. I just want to have fun with my friends, go to the beach, and talk about guys, but I can't because I have to make sure my family is taken care of." My heart fell into the pit of my stomach as I grit my teeth. Jesse - "Look, I cannot imagine how hard that is and how much weight you have on your shoulders, but at the end of the day, you do it because you love your family and because you want to help, and I know it's hard to see but God loves you more for that. The same way you love your family and how hard you work for them, God is working and loving you, and

He will help provide and make sure you are not alone. Look around you. This is also your family. Let us help you and make your weight become less." Youth Minister - "Alright let's wrap it up and come back to your seats. The whole group had eyes filled with tears as they got up and headed back to their seats. I began to pray asking God for guidance and how we could help this girl. The night ended and I pulled aside the youth minister. Jesse - "Hey look, in our small group today one of the girls let everyone know that she is the only one on her family that works and that they are really struggling with food and paying bills. Is there anything we can do?" Youth Minister - "Jesse, I'm sorry to say this but you're describing almost every kids' life that comes here. They are all farm workers and if the parents can't work it's the kids that help pay the bills. That's just the world in which we live in down here." She walked away as the other college students came to get me to head back to school. I couldn't help but feel helpless. What could I do to help these kids? That night I sat in the chapel praying. "God these are just kids and they live a life that an adult should be living. Lord they are filled with suffering, and anger as they wonder where you are. Lord please lead me as I do not know what to do." I sat there in silence as I leaned forward and closed my eyes. Silence is all I heard and silence is all I saw. My heart was full of pain as I prayed, "God I don't want these kids to go through what I went through. They deserve a great life Lord..." silence broke as in the depths of my heart I heard, "Share with them, share your story." "My story?" "Let your testimony be a beacon of hope for them. Let them see that anything is possible."

Chapter 9 Summer Love

Finals started and all I could think about was the summer. That summer I would be working as a camp director, I would also be leading retreats all over the U.S. and I would be going to world youth day in Brazil! As I was thinking about all that lied ahead for me, my phone buzzed in my pocket. I took my phone out. The text read, "Hey want to go to Waffle House, a bunch of people are going. - Jessica" Jesse - "Huh, I wonder why she's texting me and asking me to go?" I quickly replied - "Hey sure, just let me know when y'all are leaving." Jessica- "k we're heading out now." Jesse - "Lol, ok I'll meet y'all down stairs." I threw on some clothes, and ran down stairs to meet everyone. I waited by their dorm, as I see three girls come out. Jesse - "Hey Jessica, where is everyone else? Jessica- "Oh it's just us." Jesse - "Uh okay, let's go I'll drive." We walk towards my car as I thought, "why did she invite me if it's just them?" We get in the car as Jessica said, "yeah sorry, there was supposed to be more people, but they all bailed because they had to study." Jesse - "Who would ever say no to Waffle

House?" She laughed and said, "ya I thought of inviting you, because you're from Georgia and I know that all people from Georgia love Waffle House." Jesse - "True that." We drove off. I plugged in my phone and played some of my favorite songs. Fall Out Boy came on, so we rolled down our windows and sang. "Cuz sugar, we're going down swinging..." song after song we sang at the top of lungs. Even while we were at Waffle House all we talked about was how we had the same taste of music. The night ended in a blink of an eye and I found myself lying in my bed feeling excited about how much fun I had with her in the car. "I wonder if she likes me?" I thought. "When we get back home I should ask her if she wants to hang out. Yeah, I should definitely do that, because if she does want to hang out then maybe she does like me." I closed my eyes, as I kept thinking of her.

Finals came and went and I all of a sudden, I found myself back home. It was only a week before I had to leave for Chicago. I was sitting on the floor trying to decide what to pack as I stared at my phone. "I wonder if I should text her." "I don't know if I should, but I did tell her I would." "Uh, maybe I should..." I grabbed my phone as I began to type... Jesse - "Hey, so nice to be home huh? So we should totally grab dinner or something tomorrow." My finger hovered over the send button, as I thought "maybe this is a little too forward, maybe I should tone it down a bit." I deleted the whole message and started again, "Hey, so we should totally get some bros together and all hang out?" "Uh no," I thought, "she's going to think, I think of her only as a friend if I say bro." I deleted the whole thing again and began to type, "Hey, we should totally go to Waffle House again, because I leave in a week. Let me know when your free." Send. Boom, I jumped off the ground and my phone falls to the floor. "Dang, I sent it." "What if she is weirded out and says she can't." "Oh man she's going to think I'm weird...

"text message ring" I dive to my phone to see what she wrote. Jesse - "Ya of course, how about tomorrow?!." "Yes, yes, yes, she wants to hang out." I replied back, "Perfect, I'll pick you up tomorrow at noon." Send. I ran to my closet to look for clothes to wear. "Text message ring." Jessica - "Awesome, see you then." Jesse - "She said awesome, oh man, she must really like me!" I grabbed my blue button-down shirt and my favorite pair of jeans and threw them in the washer. "I hope this is fun tomorrow, and not awkward."

The next day came and I picked her up from her house. I made a specific playlist of songs we could jam out to. I was a bit nervous as I tried to make conversation. Jesse - "So are you happy to be home?" Jessica - "Yeah I guess so, I miss my friends back at school and stuff." Jesse - "Yeah same here, but I'm pretty excited for this summer, it's going to be awesome." Jessica- "Yeah I bet, it sounds like you're going to be doing so much stuff, my summer is going to be kind of boring. I'll be hanging around here until I get to go to South Africa to visit my family." Jesse- "Wait, what? You're going to South Africa?!?! That's so sick." "Oh hey by the way I thought we could maybe walk at this sick trail by the Chattahoochee river before we ate if that okay?" Jessica - "Yeah! That sounds amazing. I love trails." Jesse - "Okay wait so going back to where we were, you're going to South Africa?" Jessica - "Yeah, my dad is originally from there and a lot of his family is still there so we go and visit them when we can." Jesse - "That's so sick. So you're kind of like that cartoon uh... what's it called... the Wild Thornberry's!" Jessica- "Hahaha, yeah kind of." I parked my car by the trail and we began walking as Jessica asked, "well what about you?" Jesse - "Uh what do you mean?" I knew what she meant. She was asking about my family but I didn't really want to talk about it. I just met her, but at the same time I didn't want to be rude. Jessica - "Where are you and your family from?" Perfect I guess I'll just tell her where everyone is from and I don't have to be specific.

"I'm from Los Angeles, and then I moved to Georgia when I was ten years old and have been living here since." Jessica - "What about your parents?" Jesse- "Well both of my mom and dad were... uh I mean are Salvadoran." "They both met down there." Jessica- "Oh wow, that's awesome." The silence grew as a drip of sweat traveled down from the top of my neck all the way down my back. I don't know why, but I didn't want her to know I was adopted. I didn't want her to pity me. Jesse - "Wow, it's such a beautiful day huh?" Jessica - "Yeah! The trees are so green and the sound of the river flowing is so peaceful." Jesse- "Yeah, I love the color they chose for these pavers the medium gray is always my favorite way to go." Jessica - "Hahaha, you're a funny one huh?" Jess e- "It all depends on who is my audience." We came to a bench where there was a tree hanging over the river. You could look into the clear water where you couldn't tell what tree was real, the tree or its reflection. We sat down and looked across the river. Jesse - "Wow, this is great huh?" Jessica - "Hmm yeah, how do you know about this place?" Jesse - "Well I used to be a youth minister intern and I would come here and run and sometimes I would just sit here and pray. I love going to church and being at youth group but sometimes being alone here with God... I just, I don't know, haha, it's just beautiful. Jessica - "That's awesome, ya I agree, some of my favorite times in my life was when I was praying when I was little. My dad used to take me to this little chapel every Sunday and we would pray. Sometimes I drew or sometimes I would just sit there and talk to God and sometimes I would just sit there in silence. I think it was then that I really started learning more about God." Jesse - "Well that's awesome. So, I bet for you it's like having a relationship with God rather than having knowledge about him?" She leaned in and her hand slightly touched mine as she said "Yes, exactly! It was always a relationship and I think that's what so many people miss." Jesse - "I one million times agree with you." Jesse – "I went to this youth group once where a kid knew more theology than me, but he didn't know God, he just knew more about him. And for me, yes, those things are important, but I think it's better to know God, to be able to know his laughter, his smile, his disappointment, his pain, and his tears. I feel like that's how we should all know God. The water in the river kept running, and people walked by as the sun began to set. Jesse - "Man I'm pretty hungry, how about you?" Jessica - "Yeah I'm starving." I pulled out my phone, "No way dude! It's 5pm!" Jessica - "Wait what?" Jesse - "yeah it's 5pm! Hahaha." We both laughed as we got up and headed back to the car. Jessica - "So I guess we should go to Waffle House now huh?" I plugged in my phone and the music began to play. It was Waffle House part two. Darkness covered the sky as I dropped her off. The roads were lit with street lights and the road looked endless. I thought to myself, "I don't know what just happened, all I know is I am excited." I got home and quickly texted her "Hey, had so much fun today!" Jessica - "Me too! Let's hang out next week again?!?!" I began to type, "Yeah that would be..." oh no... I'm not going to be here." Dang it I totally forgot about Chicago and this summer. I texted her, "Yeah well maybe a little bit sooner than that, because I leave for Chicago next week." Jessica - "Oh yeah, I forgot. How about tomorrow then?" Jesse - "Yeah, tomorrow is perfect. I had so much fun today I really cannot wait!" Jessica - "Me too, see you tomorrow!" I laid in bed thinking about the whole day. I stared at my ceiling as I tried to make sense of all of it. "Don't get your hopes up," I told myself, "You're going to Chicago and are going to be super far away, and it's just not going to work." I rolled over to my side as I closed my eyes and thought, I can always hope.

We hung out the next day with a couple friends and we were all laughing and playing card games. I felt like I was watching a movie and all I could do was watch the main actress. Her laugh, the way she brushed her hair behind her ear, the way her cheeks grew red when she was embarrassed, and the way she radiated joy. Jessica - "Hey Jesse, it's getting late, I better be getting back now." Jesse - "Uh yeah it is. We better get going." I didn't want the night to end. I hugged my friend's goodbye as they all wished me good luck in Chicago. As we walked towards my car Jessica quickly said, "it's going to be weird not being able to hang out with you." I reached over and held her hand as I held tightly and looked at her and said, "you'll only be a call away."

Chi-Town

I have to start off by saying that Chicago is one of the coolest cities I've ever been to. Their train systems actually gets you places, their skyline is out of this world, you can drink a beer on one of the tallest buildings, and the lakes cool you off during the heat of the summer. Camp started right away once I got to Chicago. We were north of the city in a great open field with two main buildings. This is the place where I would spend half of the summer. Days were filled with workshops, Church, games, and lessons. Each night as the campers all went to sleep, I would sneak down stairs to one of the main rooms and call Jessica back home. We seemed to be getting closer and closer each day. We began sending each other books and music, and I would write letters to her detailing how amazing this book was or how moving a song was. After one of us received a letter, we would talk about it almost all night. The only thing that I could think about at camp, was if a letter would come today and when would I be able to talk to her again. Our conversations grew in depth, and I started to wonder if this would turn out to be something more than just friends. One night I snuck down stairs and called her. We struck up a conversation on a book that she had read and that I had just finished reading called, *Kisses from Kate*. Jesse - "Hey Jess, how's everything in Atlanta?! Jessica - "It's great, but did you finish *Kisses from Kate* yet?" Jesse - "Ya!!! That's why I'm calling you. I mean what a book! I can't believe that she left at such a young age to serve as a missionary." Jessica- "Ya, and what was even more amazing was her faith in God and how she literally became a mother to everyone in the village there." Jesse - "I know, as I read it, it reminded me of all the mission trips that I've gone on. I remember all the kids we would play with and help feed, and I don't know, reading it, made me miss it." Have you ever gone on a mission trip? Jessica - "No I've never been on one, but that's something I really want to do! I've been to South Africa and Rome, but I've unfortunately have never gone on a mission trip." Jesse - "Oh man we have to go on one together one day! Maybe, Jamaica? I've been there and know all the brothers and sisters, oh, and this little old man named George, he's blind but I know he will remember me from our conversations about God!" Jessica- "Hahaha. Yeah! Oh my gosh, I would love that." Jesse - "So I know that this is always a question that is hard to answer but I'm going to ask it anyway. How did you come to have such a deep faith?"

Jessica- "Well I grew up Catholic and went to church but, ever since I was a little girl, my dad would take me to this little chapel every Sunday night to pray. Sometimes my other family members would come along, but it was mostly just me and my dad. Every Sunday night, no matter what, we would go to that chapel and pray. I would sometimes write in my journal or draw, read the Bible or another book, or I would simply just sit there and talk to God. I knew that this was God and that He loves me with an incredible, powerful, and deep love. It may not show at times, but my relationship with God, is the number one most important thing in my life." Jesse - "Wow, so you're not an atheist that's good to know... "hahaha, I'm just kidding." She laughed. It was nice to know that she had a sense of humor. Jesse - "But on a serious note, that is awesome. I'm literally blown away by what you said. I would have never thought all that about you. Not saying that you do not seem like a Christian, but I don't know... does that make sense." Jessica - "Well yeah, I think it's something's that I am not so outspoken about. I keep my faith close to me, because it's so important to me." Jesse - "Yeah that makes sense." Jessica - "What about you?" Jesse - "Well I think we have a lot of similarities in our faith, but I think ours paths that got us there were very different." Jessica - "What do you mean?" Jesse - "Well for me, I've always been so angry at God, my mom left us when I was six, and my dad died when I was thirteen. So I've always believed and knew about God, but it was so hard for me to understand why God would take my family away from me and why he would allow such bad things to happen to a little kid." Jessica- "Wow Jesse, I'm so sorry. I had no idea. You always have a smile on your face and seemed okay, I would have never known...." Jesse - "Yeah it's something that I keep close to me and try not to share much." Jessica - "So how do you get from all that suffering to being in Chicago leading a Christian retreat?" Jesse - "great question, hahaha. Honestly, I was in such a low place and I found myself praying on my knees one day asking God to leave me alone and to stop causing me so much pain and suffering in my life, but I don't know how to explain it. I knew God wanted to do something great in my life, but I needed to allow him to do it and I needed to put forth an effort. So, I literally said, "God I give you two weeks and then I'm done." Those two weeks turned into a month and that month turned into a year and I have never looked back." Jessica "Wow so in those initial two weeks what happened?" Jesse - "I got invited to bible studies, book studies, and to help lead a retreat and then finally, to become a missionary for a year. "I experienced so much healing and found myself and it changed my life. "It took me a year to realize that it is not God that causes our pain, but that He instead holds us and never let's go. I think about it like a wound. A parent cannot prevent their kid from going out and getting a cut on their knee from playing outside, but what does the parent do when their kid gets hurt? The parent holds them, heals their wound, and let's them know that they love them and that they will be okay." That's what I learned, that God wasn't causing my suffering but rather He was holding me and giving me Band-Aids and holding me in his arms, singing to me and letting me know that He loves me and that I am going to be okay.

Chapter 10   Joy

Summer flew by, but my heart stayed in Georgia. I counted down the days until I would be back. My bags were packed with my flight ticket in hand as I thought back on all the phone calls and letters I've exchanged with Jessica. "I hope this is real," I thought. The whole plane ride I tried to sleep, but all I could think about was the worst possible scenario, "what if she forgot what I looked like, what is she hates how I smell, what if she only likes on the phone?" Thoughts streamed across my mind as I looked out the window. Wow, I really like her and I hope she's not as nervous as I am. The plane landed and I texted her, "Hey, just landed. Meet me outside." Jessica - "Great, see ya soon." I looked at my phone, "great, see ya soon," that's it? I'm overthinking things way too much right now. I stopped by Starbucks and picked us up coffee and headed outside. She was in a rustic silver 2006 Honda Civic. I saw her there and caught her eye and remembered back to when I first saw her in college. Her cheeks flushed red as she quickly looked down. "Oh man she's nervous too," I thought. She jumped out of the car and gave me a big hug. "How… how was your flight?" she asked." Jesse - "Hey it was great, can't complain." I threw my stuff in the back of the car and asked, "hey can I drive?" Jessica - "Sure." She tossed me the keys. I got into the car and played a playlist that I had just created. She looked over and smiled as Fall Out Boy came on, and we began singing at the top of our lungs. Song after song we kept singing just like we were back in college. We finally got to my parents' house and Jessica looked over and said, "I'm nervous." Jesse - "No don't be, it'll be fine." We ate quickly at my parents' house. I told everyone sorry that we had to leave so soon, but that I had a huge surprise for

Jessica, so we better get going. We backed out of the driveway as Jess nervously looked at me and asked, "a surprise, huh? What is it?" I kept looking out the window at the lowering sun. Jesse - "Uhhh you'll see, hahaha." We pulled up to a park. Jessica looked around and asked, "what's this? Why is everyone here." Jesse - "hahaha I told you, you'll see!" We parked our car and walked over to where all my friends were sitting. Jesse - "Hey guys this is Jessica." Jessica- "Hey guys, um can someone tell me what's going on here, because Jesse won't." Friend - "You didn't tell her? That's mean man, haha." I looked over at Jessica and saw her face shift over to worry. Jesse - "So today is August Fourth." Jessica - "Okay?" Jesse - "So on the fourth of July there is always a huge firework display, but since it rained all day this year, they moved the show to today. So, since we didn't get to spend the fourth of July together, now we do." Her face lit up as she grabbed my hand and said, "you're so sneaky Jesse." We sat down together on the grass as the announcer came on over the loud speakers and shouted, "who's ready to see the show?! We all shouted and screamed "yes!!!!!"" "Woooooooo!!!" Announcer - "Well count down with me." Five, four, three, two, one, boooooooom! Fireworks blasted off the ground and lit the night sky with sparkling lights. I looked over at Jessica and said, "this is pretty cool huh?" Jessica - "Ya, this is crazy, there's so many fireworks. It's so beautiful." Jesse - "Ya, this is pretty awesome." I scooted closer to Jessica and said, "It's good to be back, I missed you." She smiled and said, "I missed you too." The thirty-minute show seemed to pass way too fast, and I wished it was longer. We got into the car. Jesse - "Hey Jessica, everyone is going to Waffle House now, want to go?" Jessica - "No, I don't think I can. I wish I could, but it's been a long day you know." Jesse - "Yeah it really has been. You met my parents, and my friends and that's a lot hahaha." Jessica- "Yeah, I had a lot of fun tonight. Thanks Jesse for everything. It was like the best day ever! I'm so glad you're back." Jesse - Yeah it's been awesome! Thanks for picking me up from the airport and coming with me." She dropped me back off at my house. I leaned down by her window, and boldly asked, "well maybe I can see you tomorrow?" Jessica - "Maybe, if you're lucky," she said with a wink. I waved goodbye as she drove off and little did she know that fireworks were still going off in my soul."

Once Upon a Rainy Day

Days with Jessica were always filled with laughter and every night as we said goodbye to each other my heart would pull me in closer and closer. One night I laid in bed, tossing and turning and all I could think about, was Jessica. I've gotten to the place where I can't imagine life without her. I think it's time, I thought to myself. "I'm going to ask her to be my girlfriend." That morning I jumped out my bed and headed toward the kitchen. I looked over to my adopted mom and said "so I kind of need a cake, and uh maybe it should be shaped as a heart." Adopted mom - uh ok what for? Jesse - "it's for jess in going to ask her out!" Adopted mom - "Aww that's great, what's your plan?! Jesse - plan... hmmm, yes, I have that. "Plan? Shoot I need a plan." I ran back upstairs and looked for local concerts and saw that parachute was that night and quickly bought tickets. I texted Jessica and asked, "hey you still good to hang out tonight?!?! :)" a couple minutes later she responded, "yup just come pick me up!" Jesse - "sweet! It's going to be a fun night." I ran back down stairs and my adopted mom was mixing flour in eggs in a bowl. Ok so plan is to bake this cake, go to a fancy dinner, go to a concert and then walk around the river! Boom! Right?!? Adopted mom – "Yeah that's sounds fun!" Sure does! The cake was a heart shaped with pink frosting and m&ms outlined as a smaller heart on the cake. Man, she's going to love this. As I looked at it I began thinking "how am I going to ask her? What am I going to say."? I sat outside the porch swing and began thinking more and more. Why do I like jess? I like her laughter, I like her smile, but most of all I like that she feels like a lost old friend and every time I see her. Every time I see her my days gets a little better.

That night I packed the cake in the car and start driving to her house. Jesse "I somehow have to sneak the cake in her house. She can't know it's a heart shape cake or she will know that I'm going to ask her out tonight." I get to her house and I hold the cake with my right hand hidden behind my back. I knock on the door and her mother comes to the door. "Perfect." Hey Mrs. Dunwoody where jess." Dunwoody "oh she's getting ready, perfect, look so I baked her a cake but I don't want her to see it until later tonight can we hide it in your fridge? Dunwoody " - of course here let me go do that right now. She opens the refrigerator and looks around to see where it would fit, as Jessica walks out of her room. Jessica - "hey you're here!" She shouts as her mother shuts the refrigerator. Jesse - "Yup, I'm here! You ready to go?" Jessica "yeah I'm all set." "Alright mom see ya later!" Dunwoody - "bye have a fun night!" We walk out as I exhale "whew what a day" Jessica - "yeah? What's you do tonight." Jesse - "uhh not much." "Are you hungry?!" There's this awesome place we're going to! Jessica - "yeah I'm pretty hungry, so what are we doing tonight?" Jesse – "Oh, you'll see dinner first." We got in the car and began jamming out but I started singing so much that we ended up lost. My GPS for some reason kept closing and we couldn't find the restaurant. Jesse - "dude so sorry I don't know what's up with my phone today. Jessica - "no worries We can just stop any where to eat I'm not that picky." Jesse - "ok well let's see this looks like an ok restaurant." Jessica - "yeah looks nice! Jesse - "perfect let's eat." We walked in as the sound of classical music began to play. Hostess - "Hello is it for a party of two?" Jesse - yes ma'am just a party of two. Hostess - "what name is your reservation under?" Jesse - "uh no reservation just wondering if you had any seats available." She looks down on her sheet and began to count. I look over to Jessica and say "I don't know why she's counting all the tables are empty." Hostess - "ah yes one available follow me." We sat down as Jessica looked over and said "wow this is really fancy." Jesse - "yeah I know, I rented out the whole restaurant so it could be just me and you." She laughed as we both began to look over the menu. We ordered a couple beer and ate probably the most expensive dinner in the world but amazing at the same time. Jesse - "ok are you ready for surprise number two? Jessica - "yes!" "We're going to see parachute in concert!" It starts in 30 minutes right down the road." Jessica - "no way I'm so excited! Let's go" we get to the concert at the perfect time. The doors are open and People are running in. Jessica - " let's go, let's go so we can get a good seat." We run out of the car and onto the Venue. Jesse - "Front stage two rows back, this is not bad good job Jessica!" I looked over and put my shoulder around her and said I'm glad we met! Jessica - " haha me too me too." The music started blaring as we sang along at the top of our lungs. Jessica - "they are so good live huh? Jesse - "yeah they are amazing!" The concert flew by as we slowly walked out with the crowd. So, last surprise is a walk by the river and some dessert! Jessica -

"man you really planned this out huh?" Jesse - "uh something like that. I grew nervous as we drove off and got closer to the river. I began to question and wondered if she would say yes." Jessica - "wow look at the moon it's so bright and big." "And the stars, they are amazing! Jesse - "wow it's such a clear night but looks like some clouds are rolling in over there." We got there as I locked the doors and we began to walk around the river. Jesse - "So Jess it's been so amazing getting to know you, I've enjoyed our letters back and forth, I loved our laughter at 2am, and most of all I've really enjoyed your company. Jessica -" aw you're so sweet, I've really enjoyed it too. I think back and can't believe it's only been three months I feel like I've known you forever!" Jesse - "I know! I feel the same way but most of all I love how I can be myself with you." Jessica - "totally agree! "Looks there's a swing over there we should stop and sit." We sat down as my palms began to sweat. Sweat starting crawling down my back and I wondered if this was a good time to ask her." Rumbles broke my thoughts as I looked over to Jessica and said "I swear that was me." Jessica - "hahaha I know that was weird it must be thunder." Jessica - "so what was your favorite part about today?" Jesse - "honestly my favorite part was the restaurant." "Even though I really messed up I was glad you were so cool about it." "What about you?" Jessica - "hmm I think my favorite part was the concert. They were good." Jesse -"yeah they were so good." Jesse - "Jessica you know what I like about you?" Jessica - "what?" Jesse - "I like your laughter, I like that you call vans busses, I like that squinty look you give me when you don't get my jokes, and I like simply being with you. It's been a really fun time and I want to keep this adventure going. So Jessica will you be my girlfriend?" I looked over as her cheeks grew closer to her eyes. She quickly raised her voice - Jessica "Jesse I would love to be your girlfriend!" I leaned over and gave her a kiss as a wet drop fell on the top of my head. Jesse - "so either a bird pooped on my head or is that rain?" Jessica - "no I felt a drop too. I think it's rain." One after another rain began to pour. We looked up as what was a beatific night became a sleet of rain covering the sky. We both laughed so hard by the time we got up we were completly soaked. Jessica - "let's go back to the car." Jesse - "yeah great idea." We rain back as the rain feel harder and harder. We jumped into the car as we both looked at each other wondering what just happened. Jesse – "So either you becoming my girlfriend is a really bad idea of God is trying to be funny and give us a Nicholas Sparks moment?" Jessica "Hahaha gosh I don't know but I'm so happy you asked me. It took you long enough."

Since the day I met her I knew she was the one and only two years later would she officially become my wife.

Chapter 11 Truth, Beauty, & Goodness

I was summer of 2011 and I was flying back from a leadership camp. The plane was filled with everyone that I met at the camp, so of course the plane became rowdy with Conversation about God, testimonies, philosophy, and etc. I boarded the plane and sat down hoping someone I knew from the conference would be seated next to me. Person after person walked by until this older man boarded and sat right next to me. "Man" I thought, "I should have grabbed my headphones from my suitcase." The man sat down and of course I said hello and he was polite, and we began talking about our trips. Jesse - "so were you here for business or just visiting? Man - "no I was here for business." Jesse - "oh wow, what do you do?" Man - "I do air traffic control and I had to come and train some people here so now I'm going home." Jesse - "wow air traffic control so what does that entail and how did

you get into that, if you do not mind me asking?"
Man - "so I enlisted in the army and that is where I
learned." "I worked in the air traffic division when I
was overseas." Jesse - "that's so cool I bet it's a
huge difference compared to the states." Man - "oh
yeah just a couple risk factors but really not that
difficult." Man - "so what brought you here?" Jesse
- "great questions, so I'm currently a missionary
and I helped with a retreat this weekend that helps
teenagers become leaders in their own community."
Man - "oh so you must be Christian or something."
"I hate Christians." Jesse - "uhhhh.. ok, why do you
say that." Man - "honestly I just don't get it, I just
hate God, I don't believe in him and I never will."
Jesse - "but that doesn't make sense, you can't just
say you hate God and not have a reason, so what's
the reason?" His posture changed as he crossed his
harms and spoke quicker, Man - "I just don't know
why he created us, like what was the point? Because
life sucks so did, he create us just to suffer and be
miserable?" Jesse - "God created us out of love, and
goodness." Man - "Then why do people suffer?

Why are there people dying every day and awful things happening?" Jesse - "because God allows free will, he allows us to live with free choice and that sometimes comes with pain and suffering but also love and healing." Man - "That's just stupid, I hate Christian, it's just stupid. I would rather not be created. I don't want that love, I don't want that goodness, just leave me alone." Jesse - "why are you so angry? What happened to you that made you so angry?" Man - "I told you to leave me alone." He jumps out of his seat and headed toward the front of the plane. I looked out the window and quickly ask God, how can I help this man? Man - He grabs the flight attendant and says, "this freaking Christian, this guy, as he points to me, make him move or find me a new seat because he won't shut up." Flight attendant - she looked at me and said - "sir can you just leave this man alone, this is a full flight and I cannot move him to sit anywhere else." Jesse -" yeah, I mean I really didn't say much." Flight Attendant - "ok yeah I would just stay to yourself." Jesse - "ok..." This day is forever etched in my mind as the plane landed and the man left without a single word being added to our conversation. I remember this because I didn't just understand what he was saying, I lived it. I've felt his anger, I felt his cry, and I felt his questioning of God, but sadly I couldn't do anything about it. That's why I wrote this book, I wrote it to share my story, to share what I've seen, to share what life has thought me, and to show you that if I can do it, you can also. So, if you're like me and are lost, broken and hating life, God or whatever I challenge you to give God two weeks.

I challenge you to say - yes to truth. For two weeks ask people, why do you believe in God? What does life mean to you? Start reading books that expand your way of thinking, I started reading Francis Chan – Crazy Love and I would also suggest, The Alchemist, A grief observed, and The Problem with Pain by C.S. Lewis.

I challenge you to say - yes to beauty. Beauty comes in many different sizes and places. This challenge calls you to actually physically go. Go to a new church, go on a mission trip and live with the poor, go to California and see the waves crashing into the outer banks, go on a hike and breathe the air at the top of the highest cliff. This world is a lot bigger than you, but you have a great place in it. Go find it!

I challenge you to say - yes to goodness. Go and do something good in the world and give back. Go to the homeless shelter, go on the mission trip, go to the poor cities where you live and get to know the people. Hear their stories, where they come from, and how you could help, and sometimes it's simple as having an open ear. Seek the good of people and ask where do they find joy?

I challenge you to try something new, I challenge you to think a new way, I challenge you to see the world beyond yourself because it is only then you can begin to find meaning. This world leaves a lot of us broken, battered, snot nosed, and alone. As we grow older, we will only embody this pit the world leaves us in, unless we take a stand. That's what this challenge is about. This challenge is not about laying around and waiting for opportunity, a miracle, or anything to come knocking at your door. It's time to get up! I give you two weeks.

Also, I would love to hear your story. What I've come to learn is that you cannot do this without community. You can send me a message on my website – www.twoweeks.org

Epilogue

One late august afternoon I was playing during recess as laughter filled the grounds. We were playing kick ball and it was my turn. I stepped up to the plate, as the pitcher told everyone - "hey scoot in, he can't kick." My cheeks turned red and I thought to myself, "I'll show them I can kick!" The pitcher rolled the ball toward me as I got a running start and swung my leg as hard as I could. Boom! The ball shot off like a cannon. It went flying across the playground as everyone screamed "run, run" I was so distracted I forgot to run. I ran around every base as everyone cheered "Jesse, Jesse, Jesse." I rounded third and headed home as I saw my dad with the biggest grin on his cheeks. Jesse - "Dad, did you see that?! I kicked that ball and it was a home run! Dad - "Yes! I saw it, you did so good! I'm so proud of you!" He hugged me tight as I looked up and said - I thought you were at work why are you here?! Dad - I'm on my lunch break and I just wanted to stop by and see you. He got down on one knee and he said, "Jesse I am so proud to be your dad; don't you ever forget that." My dad was an amazing man and I miss him all the time. When I graduated college, when I got my first big job at Uber Corporate, when I got married, and as I look up to the night sky, I always wonder if my dad be proud of me? I will always miss my dad but now-a-days missing him is a joyful celebration of what he taught me, and who he helped me become.

Made in the USA
Monee, IL
07 April 2021